The MARTYRS of CÓRDOBA

Community and Family Conflict in an Age
of Mass Conversion

Jessica A. Coope

UNIVERSITY OF NEBRASKA PRESS

LINCOLN & LONDON

⊚ The paper in this book meets the minimum requirements of
American National Standard for Information Sciences — Permanence of
Paper for Printed Library Materials, ANSI Z39.48-1984.

Library of Congress Cataloging-in-Publication Data
Coope, Jessica A., 1958–
    The martyrs of Córdoba : community and family conflict in an age
of mass conversion / Jessica A. Coope.
        p.   cm.
    Includes bibliographical references and index.
    ISBN 0-8032-1471-5 (hard)
        1. Christian martyrs — Spain — Córdoba (Province)   2. Córdoba (Spain:
    Province) — Church History.   3. Christianity and other religions —
    Islam — History.   4. Islam — Relations — Christianity — History.
    I. Title.
    BX4659.S8C66   1995
    272 — dc20
                                                            94-30425
                                                                CIP

Contents

The original research for this book was facilitated by a grant from the Mabelle McLeod Lewis Memorial Fund. A Maude Hammond Fling Faculty Summer Fellowship from the University of Nebraska gave me the time I needed to complete the project.

I wish to thank Tom Bestul for being so generous with his time and advice during the writing of this book. Thomas Bisson, Ira Lapidus, and James Monroe all made helpful comments on an early version of the manuscript. Finally, I am grateful to Stephen Hilliard and to my parents, Ann and Fred Coope, for their love and support.

Introduction

Between 850 and 859 the Muslim government of Córdoba executed forty-eight Christians on two different charges. Most were accused of making denigrating remarks about the prophet Muhammad, which under Islamic law was a capital offense for non-Muslims. Some were Christians with one or more Muslim parent and were therefore considered under Islamic law to be Muslims; their crime was apostasy to Christianity. With few exceptions, these martyrs (as some of their Christian contemporaries called them) deliberately invited execution. Some appeared before the Muslim *qadi* (high judge) of Córdoba, proclaiming that Muhammad was a magician, an adulterer, and a liar and that his followers would certainly go to hell. Others made similar remarks on the streets of Córdoba. Christians of Muslim parentage who had kept their faith secret for years suddenly revealed themselves to friends and relatives as apostates.

About half of those killed were clergy or were living under a monastic vow at the time of their death. This movement was not, however, confined to monks, nuns, and clergy, groups one might expect to be particularly hostile to Islam. Nor were the martyrs typically people who had lived in isolation from Muslims and Islamic culture. Rather, their numbers included former civil servants in the Islamic government as well as sons, daughters, and siblings of Muslims.

The government reacted harshly to denunciations of the prophet

Muhammad and to cases of apostasy. Offenders were jailed and given a chance to recant their statements. If they refused, they were executed in public by decapitation with a sword.[1] The bodies were generally burned, displayed publicly on hooks, thrown into the river, or simply left in the street under guard. Concerned that Christians would venerate the bodies as relics and thus give legitimacy to the voluntary martyrdoms, Muslim officials made it as difficult as they could for Christians to obtain the bodies; they also wanted to demonstrate that the bodies would rot like any others and not be miraculously preserved from decay. As the martyrdoms continued, the government made life difficult for all Christians in Córdoba by arresting clergy, closing monasteries, raising Christians' taxes, and dismissing them from government service.

Not only Muslims were dismayed by the martyrs' actions. Many Christians in Córdoba saw the martyrs as fanatics and troublemakers who were disturbing the formerly relatively peaceful relationship between Christians and their Muslim rulers. Prominent Christians from both clergy and laity spoke out against the movement. At the same time, supporters of the martyrs wrote vitriolic polemical works condemning both Muslims and skeptical Christians. By the early 850s the voluntary martyrdoms had precipitated a crisis in relations between Muslims and Christians and a bitter split within the Christian community.

The martyrs' supporters understood the movement as a reaction to the horrors of Muslim rule, a radical but justifiable form of protest. In their writings they compared those executed to the early Roman martyrs and the actions of the government to the persecutions of Diocletian. The facts, however, did not fully support such a comparison. Most of those killed in Córdoba brought about their own arrest and execution; the authorities did not seek them out. It is true that non-Muslims in traditional Islamic societies did not enjoy legal equality with Muslims, and the handicaps they bore should not be minimized. Yet Islamic law viewed Christians and Jews as protected subcommunities within society and did not force them to convert. Their communities were granted considerable legal autonomy. And in Córdoba, as elsewhere in the Islamic world, Jews, Christians, and recent converts to Islam held government jobs. Although Córdoba in the mid-ninth century was far from being an egalitarian society, it is difficult to see much parallel between the situation of Christians under Islam and that during the Roman persecutions. To the extent that Muslims in Córdoba did actively persecute Christians, they did so after the martyrdoms began, not before, so that the martyrs' movement was more likely the cause of ill-treatment than a response to it. If the martyrdoms cannot be attributed to an active Muslim persecution, why did some Christians prefer death to life under Islamic rule?

The exploration of this question presents some difficulties. One is the nature of the sources. The primary accounts of the martyrdoms were written by the Cordovan priest Eulogius, who wrote biographical sketches of each martyr and polemic defending the movement and who himself died as a martyr in 859.[2] Eulogius's friend and associate the layman Paul Albar also wrote polemic in defense of the martyrs and a biography of Eulogius.[3] Other Latin and Arabic sources contribute important information about contemporary life in Córdoba and about the impact of the martyrdoms on Cordovan society; with a few exceptions, however, all the direct references to the martyrs come from Eulogius and Albar. Albar and Eulogius held identical opinions about events in Córdoba, including reverence for the martyrs and implacable hatred toward all Muslims and toward Christians who rejected the martyrs. The view of events they offer is shaped by their own very specific agenda. To what extent, then, can we trust their information? And because their interpretations of the facts are the only ones we have, how can we learn of the concerns and motivations of any of the martyrs other than Eulogius himself?

Another problem has to do with the nature of modern scholarship pertaining to medieval Spain. The field has always to some extent been split between Islamicists, who are concerned primarily with the history of the Muslims in Spain and only tangentially with the Christian subject population, and historians of Christian Spain, who have been far more interested in studying Christian communities under Islam than in examining Islamic societies as a whole. In the nineteenth century and the first half of the twentieth century, this split was highly polemicized, particularly within Spain itself.

Some Spanish scholarship of that period, although by no means all, was strongly pro-Christian and anti-Muslim. For these scholars, the Muslim occupation was a tragedy that was responsible for modern Spain's lack of political and cultural prominence in relation to the rest of Western Europe.[4] Christian communities under Islam were outposts of resistance or even the earliest centers of Spanish nationalism.[5] Christian culture under Islam was innovative and vital, while Islamic culture was shallow, derivative, and decadent.[6] In short, scholars of this persuasion held essentially the same view of Islam that Eulogius did and accepted his version of events uncritically. Islamicists of the same period, particularly those who were not Spanish, took the opposite point of view. Perhaps in reaction to Spanish scholarship, they downplayed the vitality and importance of Christian culture under Islam. If they discussed the martyrs at all, they accepted the point of view of the martyrs' Muslims and Christian opponents, dismissing them as fanatics.[7]

In the last few decades, scholars have taken a more interdisciplinary and balanced approach to the study of Muslim Spain, and the field has lost much of its polemical quality.[8] But with few exceptions, studies of the martyrs' movement have not profited from these new approaches.[9] There may be an ideological reason why the present generation of Islamicists studying Muslim Spain, who would be in a good position to place the martyrs in a historical context, have avoided the subject. Much recent scholarship has depicted medieval Islamic societies as pluralistic and tolerant of diversity in ways that are appealing to modern liberal sensibilities.[10] Eulogius and Albar, however, did not share this high valuation of Islamic society. They feared diversity. They despised anyone who did not conform to their beliefs. They believed Muslims had no right to exist and depicted them only through the most hateful stereotypes. Anyone who is attracted by the image of a diverse and tolerant medieval Islam is bound to find the martyrs and their supporters a singularly repellent group.

Any effective approach to the martyrs' movement requires the creative use of all available sources. Despite their obvious biases, Eulogius and Albar were reliable witnesses up to a point. Their intended audience included fellow Christians in Córdoba who were skeptical of the martyrs but whom Eulogius and Albar hoped to win over. Writing for neighbors and contemporaries, they were free to exaggerate, embellish, and reinterpret, but not to make up events out of whole cloth. And although very few direct references to the martyrs exist outside the works of these two authors, the general depiction they give of relations between Christians and Muslims can be confirmed by other Latin sources.[11]

Most important, the Christian authors' limited point of view can be supplemented by a study of Islamic society in ninth-century Córdoba.[12] Wherever one can juxtapose information about changes in Islamic society with Eulogius's and Albar's statements about Cordovan society and culture, it becomes clear that the authors' bitter polemic did not simply derive from bigotry or their own overheated imaginations. However hysterical their prose, they were responding to real changes. The Islamic presence in Córdoba underwent a qualitative change in the first half of the ninth century. The government grew stronger, the bureaucracy expanded, and the cultural life of the court became more vital. As a result, Christians were increasingly drawn to Arab Islamic culture, and the rate of conversions to Islam accelerated, leading to changes and disruptions at every level of Cordovan society, from government to the family. The voluntary martyrdoms can best be understood in this Islamic context; they represented an attempt to resist assimilation and conversion to Islam and to strengthen Christian identity by invoking the heroic image of the Roman martyrs.

The problem of how to separate out the motivations of individual martyrs from those of Eulogius cannot be fully resolved, but some distinctions can be made.[13] Eulogius had his own ideas about the meaning of the martyrdoms, but he was a careful biographer, and he often provides enough detail about the lives of individual martyrs to allow us to draw conclusions quite different from his own. Eulogius, for example, attributes the actions of a martyr who once worked for the Islamic government, suddenly left his job and retired to a monastery, and subsequently sought martyrdom to religious zeal. We, however, are free to speculate that a conflict with his Muslim employers may have played a role in his behavior. In addition, Eulogius was not altogether mistaken when he assumed that his beliefs and those of the other martyrs were identical. Many of those killed knew Eulogius personally, and they shared common ideals. Also, he wrote his accounts of the martyrdoms in installments, as events unfolded, so that later martyrs may well have read his works and taken on his ideas as their own. The picture that emerges from the sources is of a radical Christian movement whose leadership was made up of literate clerics and laymen like Eulogius and Albar and was centered mostly at the Cordovan monasteries and basilicas. This leadership had clearly articulated ideas of what the movement meant. Some of the martyrs came out of this group; some understood and shared its goals; and some became martyrs for personal and idiosyncratic reasons that had little to do with the leaders' goals.

The question of individual motives can never be definitively resolved, but we can understand that the group as a whole was reacting to changes in Islamic Cordovan society. Studying the martyrs allows us to explore some intriguing questions: To what extent was medieval Islamic society tolerant, and in what ways did non-Muslims perceive it as discriminatory and repressive? How did non-Muslim subject groups maintain their cultural boundaries? What exactly did it mean to be a Christian or a Muslim in the pluralistic world of ninth-century Córdoba? Was it a question of theological beliefs only? Of culture in a broader sense? Of race? By what process did each religious group form stereotypes of the other? Muslims and moderate Christians in Córdoba may have been justified in describing the martyrs as fanatics; but fanatics can articulate in heightened form their culture's most profound anxieties.

Chronology of the Martyrs' Movement

DATE	EVENT
822	Death of al-Hakam I
ca. 822	Execution of **Adulphus and John** (Muslim father, Christian mother)
848 or 850	Eulogius's journey to Pamplona
18 April 850	Execution of **Perfectus** (a priest)
ca. May 851	John the merchant beaten and jailed
3 June 851	Execution of **Isaac** (formerly *exceptor rei publicae,* later a monk at Tabanos)
June 851	Execution of **Sanctius** (a soldier in the amir's army)
7 June 851	Execution of **Peter** (a priest), **Walabonsus** (Christian father, Muslim mother), **Sabinianus** (a monk), **Wistremundus** (a monk), **Habentius** (a monk), and **Jeremiah** (a monk and cofounder of Tabanos)
16 July 851	Execution of **Sisenandus**
20 July 851	Execution of **Paul** (a relative of Eulogius)
25 July 851	Execution of **Theodemirus** (a monk)

22 October 851	Execution of **Nunilo and Alodia** (Muslim father, Christian mother)
November 851	Eulogius and Bishop Saul jailed
24 November 851	Execution of **Flora** (Muslim father and brother, Christian mother) and **Maria** (Christian father, Muslim mother)
Late 851	Eulogius refuses to say mass
851?	Eulogius elected bishop of Toledo
early 852	Episcopal council meets to discuss the martyrs
13 January 852	Execution of **Gumesindus** (a priest) and **Servus Dei** (a monk)
27 July 852	Execution of **Aurelius** (Muslim father, Christian mother), **Sabigotho (Nathalia)** (Muslim father, Christian mother and stepfather), **Felix** (raised a Christian, converted to Islam, then back to Christianity), **Liliosa** (both parents secret Christians), and **George** (a monk from Jerusalem)
20 August 852	Execution of **Christopher** (a monk and relative of Eulogius) and **Leovigildus** (a monk)
15 September 852	Execution of **Emila** and **Jeremiah**
16 September 852	Execution of **Rogellius** (a monk) and **Servus Dei** (a monk)
ca. September 852	Increased harassment of clergy under Abd al-Rahman II
22 September 852	Death of Abd al-Rahman II
Sept.–Oct. 852	Muhammad I dismisses all Christians at court, destroys churches, imposes new taxes on Christians. Bishop Saul arrested.
13 June 852	Execution of **Fandila** (a monk at Tabanos)
June 853?	Bishop Saul flees Córdoba
14 June 853	Execution of **Anastasius** (a priest), **Felix** (a monk and a Berber convert from Islam), and **Digna** (a nun at Tabanos)
15 June 853	Execution of **Benildis**

17 September 853	Execution of **Columba** (a nun at Tabanos)
19 September 853	Execution of **Pomposa** (a nun)
853?	Group swearing at which leading clergy and laymen condemn the martyrs
11 July 854	Execution of **Abundius** (a priest)
30 April 855	Execution of **Amador, Peter** (a monk), and **Louis** (a relative of Eulogius)
855?	Execution of **Witesindus** (raised a Christian, converted to Islam, back to Christianity)
17 April 856	Execution of **Helias** (a priest), **Paul** (a monk), and **Isidor** (a monk)
28 June 856	Execution of **Argimirus** (formerly *censor* of Córdoba, later a monk)
19 July 856	Execution of **Aurea** (Muslim father, Christian mother, described by Eulogius as from an Arab family)
13 March 857	Execution of **Rudericus** (a priest, one Muslim brother, one Christian brother) and **Salomon**
858	Monks Usuard and Odilard come to Córdoba, collect relics of Aurelius, Sabigotho, Felix, and George.
11 March 859	Execution of **Eulogius** (a priest) and **Leocritja** (both parents Muslims)

THE MARTYRS OF CÓRDOBA

The Islamic Background

The proper relationship of Muslims to their subject populations was one of the most difficult problems posed by the seventh- and eighth-century Arab conquests.[1] After Muhammad's death in 632 his followers were able to conquer much of the Byzantine and Sasanian empires, which were weakened by warfare with each other. The Arabs took Syria and Egypt by 643, Iraq and most of Iran by 660, and North Africa and most of Spain (with the help of a large Berber contingent) by 713. The Arab leadership did not see the conquests primarily as wars of conversion; Muslim Arabs were to be a ruling elite, supported by the tribute of an essentially undisturbed native population. Polytheists were forced to convert, but monotheists or "people of the book" (*ahl al-kitab*) could retain their religions; people of the book included Christians, Jews, and Zoroastrians. In most areas, the Muslims established garrison towns where soldiers were housed, a practice that theoretically allowed Muslims to remain isolated from the general population.

Laws pertaining to non-Muslims evolved in such a way as to maintain the separate legal status of Muslims and their subjects. Social and legal relations between Muslims and non-Muslim monotheists were controlled by a set of laws called the *dhimma;* a non-Muslim member of an Islamic society was a *dhimmi.*[2] *Dhimmi*s were tolerated in that they were entitled to certain protections; they were allowed to practice their religion and to be governed by their own laws, which in al-Andalus (the Arabic term for Muslim Spain) was Visigothic law.[3] Law was personal rather than territorial; the government could interfere in criminal matters, if Islamic law had been violated, or if a case involved a dispute between a *dhimmi* and a Muslim, but in most instances *dhimmi* communities were legally autonomous.[4] *Dhimmi*s were not tolerated, however, in that they were not regarded as equal to Muslims. They paid a special poll tax called the *jizya;* they were obliged to wear distinctive clothing; they could not preach or conduct any public displays of their religion, including funeral processions or the ringing of church bells. Theoretically, *dhimmi*s were not allowed to hold any position that would give them authority over Muslims, although in practice many Muslim rulers ignored that prohibition and employed *dhimmi*s in important administrative posts.

The garrison towns and the provisions of the *dhimma* were designed to create a stable society in which the ruling group was clearly defined and non-Muslims would not readily convert to Islam. But in the long run, this policy of maintaining a separate Arab Muslim elite, removed physically from the subject population by the garrison towns and legally by the provisions of the *dhimma,* proved impossible to sustain. The institution of the garrison town began to break down almost at once, as men grew tired of being soldiers and began to view the conquered area as their new home.[5] Muslims never did establish garrison towns in al-Andalus; there the conquerors settled in preexisting cities, including Córdoba and Seville, and it is not clear that they were ever expected to live in physical isolation from the subject population.[6] Arab Muslims were in the minority wherever they conquered, and they arrived lacking many of the administrative and cultural skills necessary to rule an empire. They needed trained Jewish and Christian and Zoroastrian bureaucrats to help them govern, and the resulting contact made it inevitable that they would absorb elements of the indigenous populations' culture. Arab Muslims soon adopted and developed uniquely Islamic versions of Byzantine and Sasanian administration, art, and architecture, of Persian literature, of Greek philosophy, and of Christian and Jewish theology and ascetic practices.[7] Cultural borrowing worked the other way as well. The rules of the *dhimma* offered protection to non-Muslims, but they were also designed to remind non-Muslims of their second-class status, which is especially clear in rules concerning etiquette; if a Muslim and a *dhimmi* met in a narrow street, for example, the *dhimmi* must step aside and make room for the Muslim. Non-Muslims, therefore, particularly if they lived near a center of Muslim administration, had strong incentives to adopt the dress, manners, language, and eventually the religion of their conquerors.

Not all cultural changes occurred at the same pace. The garrison system broke down within decades of the initial conquests, if not sooner. Conversion of the subject populations to Islam, however, was a slow process that did not reach its peak in the Middle East and al-Andalus until the tenth or eleventh century, and Islamic empires through Ottoman times maintained substantial non-Muslim minorities. The nature of interactions between rulers and subjects also varied from place to place; the Arab conquerors borrowed very heavily from Persian high culture, for example, but much less from Latin high culture in al-Andalus. Even within one geographic area, social relations could be more or less stable in different periods so that Christians and Jews in al-Andalus were more likely to convert (or even emigrate) under the fundamentalist Almoravid (1086–1147) and Almohad (1156–1212) regimes than under earlier, more tolerant Muslim rulers. Despite the many variations, however, the basic phenomenon was the same: the system of the *dhimma* was designed to maintain a stable, pluralized society with a clearly defined ruling elite. But the interdependence and proximity of Muslims and *dhimmi*s meant that cultural boundaries between groups were never so rigid as theory dictated, and a gradual process of acculturation took place.[8]

The word "acculturation" implies a process of mutual change, but in practice in any given situation the extent of cultural borrowing is rarely equally balanced. I believe that the 850s in Córdoba were so turbulent because whatever balance had existed between Christians and Muslims was fairly suddenly upset in favor of Arab Muslim culture. The increasing wealth and stability of the Umayyad regime in al-Andalus made Arab Muslim culture a more powerful force in the mid-eighth century than it had been previously. Christians were affected in several ways: they found that it was to their financial and social advantage to adopt elements of Arab Muslim culture, including Arab Muslim dress and the practice of circumcision; they were increasingly attracted to the Arab literary tradition; and they were increasingly likely to convert to Islam. This is not to say that cultural borrowing moved in only one direction in ninth-century Córdoba, but what happened there begins to look less like mutual acculturation and more like assimilation—that is, a one-way cultural shift pulling Christians into Arab Muslim culture.[9]

There are no records of conversions that provide exact numbers to support this theory. The supposition that the rate of conversion accelerated in the mid-ninth century can be generally supported, however, by juxtaposing the history of the Umayyad regime in this period, a story of increasing wealth and cultural flowering, with the outrage of Christian writers such as Eulogius and Albar in their denunciations of fellow Christians who converted to Islam or embraced Arab Muslim culture. In this context the martyrs' movement can be read as an effort to circle the wagons, to reassert the superiority of Latin high culture and of Christianity as a religion.

The shift in relative cultural power in Córdoba grew out of the new success of the Umayyad government after 800. Before that point Muslim rulers in al-Andalus had had to direct most of their resources toward containing civil wars and factionalism. Once the amirs had achieved some political stability in the early ninth century, however, they found that they had the leisure and the tax revenues from subdued provinces to expand their administration and to take a greater interest in such courtly luxuries as literature, philosophy, music, and fashion. Young men, Christians and Jews as well as Muslims, were drawn to the palace as a place where they might find intellectual stimulation, a lucrative post, or at the very least a party furnished with fine wines and fashionable poets and musicians. The Umayyads were no longer simply an occupying military force but a cultural and economic force as well.

The Cordovan government achieved its stability only after more than a century of struggles. When the Muslim governor of Africa, Musa ibn Nusayr, and his general Tariq ibn Ziyad invaded Spain in 711, they encountered little resistance.[10] The original invading force—which arrived in two waves—totaled about twelve thousand men, the majority of whom were Berbers under the command of a small elite of Syrian Arabs. Under the loose supervision of the Umayyad caliphate at Damascus, the conquest was quickly completed, reaching as far north as Saragossa by 713.

Visigothic Spain fell easily to the conquerors because it faced internal problems: disputes within the royal family led to frequent internal warfare, and the loyalty of many elements of the population could not be counted upon. Visigothic control had never been strong in the far north, for example,[11] and city-dwellers of the Iberian Peninsula disliked the Visigoths because they did nothing to facilitate trade or the development of urban areas and because they persecuted the economically important Jewish merchants.[12] Regional conflicts, the issue of succession to the throne, and the decline of urban life presented problems for all of the Germanic kingdoms that replaced the western Roman Empire; one can imagine that a similar invasion would have made equally short work of Merovingian Gaul.

The easy defeat of the Visigoths did not guarantee that the Muslim invaders would be able to create a solid base of support for themselves. They had to contend first with an ethnic split in their ranks between Berbers and Arabs. The Arabs quickly settled in towns near the best land, particularly in the Guadalquivir valley (the government capital was originally in Seville but was shifted to Córdoba in 717). Although there were certainly some early Berber settlers in the urban south and more who arrived after 750, Berbers settled mostly in mountainous areas because many were accustomed to such terrain and because the Arabs had taken all of the good valley land.[13] Only recently converted to Islam and at that time mostly non-Arabic-speaking, the Berbers did not have a great deal in common with their Syrian Arab leaders, and they resented Arab privilege. They launched a series of revolts, often with the assistance of the indigenous population, which were to plague the early rulers of al-Andalus.

Factionalism among the Arabs themselves was another serious problem.[14] Arabic sources attribute most factionalism immediately after the conquests to long-standing tribal rivalries, but recently historians have suggested that other factors were at work as well: disputes between those who favored a policy of continued military conquest and those who favored demilitarization, for example, or between the first wave of conquerors and later arrivals.[15] One of the most dramatic such confrontations in al-Andalus took place in 741 between the early conquerors and several thousand Syrian Arab troops who had been called in to help suppress a Berber uprising. After quelling the uprising, the troops refused to go back to Syria and instead marched on Córdoba and installed their own general as governor.[16]

During the early decades of Muslim rule in al-Andalus, a succession of governors representing the Umayyad caliphate struggled for control over diverse and uncooperative ethnic and political groups. That situation changed in 750, when the Damascus-based Umayyads were overthrown by a coalition of groups who were discontented with Syrian Arab domination and with what they perceived to be the Umayyads' inability to provide religious leadership.[17] The new caliphal dynasty, the Abbasids, drew most of their support from eastern areas, particularly the Iranian province of Khurasan, and soon moved the Muslim capital east to Baghdad. The Umayyads still had powerful Arab supporters in al-Andalus, however, who invited the Umayyad prince Abd al-Rahman, one of the few Umayyad survivors of the Abbasid revolution, to come to al-Andalus.[18] Once in al-Andalus, he and his supporters took advantage of the disorganized political situation to capture Córdoba. In 756 Abd al-Rahman declared himself amir, or commander, of al-Andalus, indicating that he ruled in his own right and not as someone else's governor or delegate. He and his successors ruled until 1031, in defiance of the Abbasid caliphs.

The reign of Abd al-Rahman II (822–52) represents a turning point at which the Umayyads can first be said to have ruled a more or less united al-Andalus.[19] Abd al-Rahman's father, al-Hakam, had subdued most of the provincial revolts, resulting in a corresponding increase in provincial tax revenues. The Abbasids, who had periodically supported Arab revolts against the Cordovan regime, now faced serious problems at home and could no longer indulge in covert operations against the Umayyads. Abd al-Rahman II took advantage of this unprecedented peace and prosperity to begin raising the level of his administration and his court toward that of the Abbasids'. He introduced more specialized offices at court, along the lines of Abbasid administration. He established a central mint; before his reign most coins in circulation were from North Africa or the Abbasid east. He was the first amir to limit his public appearances, favoring the image of a distant, Hellenistic-style ruler (the image the Abbasids cultivated under Persian influence) over the more egalitarian style of traditional Arab leadership.[20] His reign saw the first exchange of ambassadors between al-Andalus and Byzantium; the Greeks now considered the Umayyads worth taking seriously and recognized that they would be natural allies against the Abbasids.

Poets, musicians, and philosophers now frequented Córdoba, and the court's demand for luxury items such as jewels and spices soared. At one point the amir purchased, at considerable expense, a necklace that had belonged to one of the wives of the Abbasid caliph Harun al-Rashid. Abd al-Rahman was eager to import Abbasid style to Córdoba, and he was willing to pay for it.

One of the amir's most influential imports was the famous singer and musician Ziryab, who had been in residence at the courts of both Baghdad and Khairouan.[21] Ziryab arrived in al-Andalus with his family and entourage in the early 820s, an event that seems to have had as powerful an impact, if on a smaller scale, as the Beatles' arrival in America. Abd al-Rahman was entranced by his new acquisition and insisted that the singer sit at his side at court and address him as an equal. In addition to influencing the musical tastes of Córdoba's elite, Ziryab introduced them to deodorant, laundry whiteners, and more sanitary serving trays for dinner parties; he taught them complex rules as to which colors and cuts of clothing were appropriate to each season; his hairstyle became a badge of good taste among courtiers. Ziryab was an educated man, knowledgeable about astronomy and geography, and he made it fashionable to be well-read in a variety of fields. As the Muslim historian al-Maqqari wrote in summing up Ziryab's influence, "Rulers and great people took him for a pattern of manners and education."

This cultural flourishing of the Umayyad court provides a context for one of the radical Christians' main complaints: that Christians were dazzled by the wealth of the Umayyad court and the financial opportunities it offered. Eulogius describes Córdoba under Abd al-Rahman as follows:

> Córdoba, however, once called Patricia, now called the Royal City, because of his [Abd al-Rahman's] residence, has been exalted by him above all, elevated with honors, expanded in glory, piled full of riches, and with great energy filled with an abundance of all the delights of the world, more than one can believe or express. So much so that in every worldly pomp he exceeds, surpasses, and excels the preceding kings of his race. And meanwhile the church of the orthodox groans beneath his most grievous yoke and is beaten to destruction.[22]

According to Albar, many Christians were eager to obtain their share of the court's wealth:

> And when we delight in their verses and in their thousand fables and even pay a price to serve them and to go along with them in their most evil deeds, and we hereby lead a life in the world and gorge our bodies, gathering together from the unlawful service and execrable ministry abundant riches, jewels, perfumes, and a wealth of clothes and different

things, making provisions far into the future for ourselves, our sons, and our grandsons . . . do we not openly bear the name of the beast in our right hand when our feelings are such?[23]

The writings of the radical Christians abound with stories intended to vilify Christians who worked for the government, who, they report, collected taxes from and otherwise abused fellow Christians and fell into the gluttony, drunkenness, and other forms of depravity typical of Muslims. Albar and Eulogius understood the martyrdoms as a reaction to the seduction of Christians by Islamic Córdoba. The martyrs defied the Muslim authorities, thus demonstrating that true Christians did not serve infidels. And through their ascetic practices, they defined Christian purity in opposition to the sensuality and luxury of the court. To underscore this opposition, Eulogius and Albar often refer to Muslims as gentiles, that is, as people living according to the body and knowing nothing of spiritual values.

Another temptation posed by the Muslims, according to Albar, was the attraction of Arabic letters:

What trained person, I ask, can be found today among our laity who with a knowledge of holy scripture looks into the Latin volumes of any of the doctors? Who is there on fire with evangelical love, with love like that of the prophets, like that of the apostles? Do not all the Christian youths, handsome in appearance, fluent of tongue, conspicuous in their dress and action, distinguished for their knowledge of Gentile lore, highly regarded for their ability to speak Arabic, do they not all eagerly use the volumes of the Chaldeans, read them with the greatest interest, discuss them ardently, and collecting them with great trouble, make them known with every praise of their tongue, the while they are ignorant of the beauty of the Church and look with disgust upon the Church's rivers of paradise as something vile?[24]

Albar may be exaggerating the extent of Christian disaffection from Latin learning, but he is pointing to something real: Christians in al-Andalus were absorbing Arabic high culture, but Muslims were not absorbing Latin high culture.

This is not to say that cultural borrowing worked only in one direction. Popular Romance poetry influenced popular Arabic poetry; it also influenced the *muwashshahat,* a more formal type of Arabic poetry, although scholars disagree as to exact relationship between Romance poetry and the *muwashshahat*.[25] There is also good evidence that Romance was widely spoken as an informal language. Christians and converts to Islam continued to use it, and most Arabs appear to have learned it as well, so that although Ibn Hazm mentions an Andalusi Arab family whose members spoke exclusively Arabic, he clearly regards them as unusual and noteworthy.[26]

Nor would it be fair to say that Latin education in Córdoba had withered away by the 850s. In Visigothic times, urban basilicas served as schools for boys who were destined for the priesthood; that tradition survived in Córdoba under Muslim rule.[27] There is some evidence of lay literacy in the Visigothic period, especially among the nobility, and Paul Albar's status as an educated layman indicates that this tradition had also survived.[28] Albar's complaint that the Christian laity of Córdoba preferred Arabic letters implies that at an earlier date they might reasonably have been expected to study Latin. It is true that Albar tells us with great excitement that Eulogius obtained a copy of the *City of God* while in northern Spain, suggesting that the range of Latin works available in Córdoba had serious limitations;[29] yet radical Christian authors had access to other of Augustine's works, as well as to works by Ambrose, John Cassian, Jerome, Gregory the Great, Prudentius, and Isidore of Seville.[30]

Yet although Latin letters continued to be studied in Córdoba and the influence of informal Romance culture remained strong, Latin high culture was losing ground: Christians studied Arabic letters, but Muslims did not integrate Latin letters into the Arabic tradition. For most Cordovan Christians, this draining of interest toward Arabic and away from Latin was probably not of great importance. But for clerics and laymen who defined themselves as scholars of Christian and Latin literature, the new dominance of a foreign cultural tradition was devastating.

Eulogius's and Albar's polemic was designed in part to counteract this trend; they glorify Latin Christian literature and denounce Christians who are drawn to Arabic letters. The martyrs believed they were protesting, in part, the loss of traditional Latin Christian high culture.

The worst fear of the radicals was that Christians would not only work for Muslims and read Arabic literature but would eventually convert to Islam; a man who associated too long with Muslims was liable to turn into one himself. Eulogius and others cite cases of Christians working at court who converted for political reasons, and Eulogius claims that many Christians converted as a result of the wave of government persecutions touched off by the martyrdoms.

The sources give only anecdotal information about conversion to Islam in the early centuries of Islamic rule. The closest anyone has come to a numerical analysis of conversion is Richard Bulliet, who has used Arabic biographical dictionaries from the period to examine the rate at which families in various areas began to adopt Muslim names.[31] His research suggests that about 20 to 30 percent of the population of al-Andalus were Muslims by 850, 50 percent by 961, and over 90 percent by 1200.[32] Bulliet maintains, though, that conversion rates were never spread evenly over the entire population of a given region. According to his theory, the earliest waves of conversion took place in the cities and especially near centers of Islamic administration. The very earliest converts in those areas faced considerable discrimination, both from their former coreligionists and from Arab Muslims who regarded converts as inferiors. A slightly later group, however, whom Bulliet calls the "early majority"—people who converted in the decades leading up to the 50 percent mark—faced less discrimination and enjoyed more advantages from their new religious status. Those converts tended to be ambitious urban men who wanted to find places for themselves in government or in the professional or business world of the Islamic cities. For al-Andalus, Bulliet classifies as early majority those people who converted between the early ninth century and the mid-tenth century; so that the martyrs' movement falls within the early majority period.

Bulliet's theory does not yield firm statistical information about conversions in al-Andalus, but his ideas combined with the anecdotal accounts in contemporary sources make possible some reasonable hypotheses. First, even if conversions overall in al-Andalus had resulted by 850 in a population that was only 20 percent Muslim, that percentage was likely to be higher in Córdoba, a large city and the center of Muslim administration. Second, those who were most likely to convert in Córdoba in the mid-ninth century were male, ambitious, and sufficiently well-educated to have reasonable hopes of succeeding in government, business, or professional life. Here Bulliet's model is a good match for the converts described by Latin and Arabic contemporary sources: ambitious, upwardly mobile, literate enough to become proficient in Arabic. Third, if Bulliet is correct that conversions were stimulated in part by economic opportunities in urban areas, then it is likely that the expansion of Umayyad administration and the growing wealth of Córdoba led to an accelerated rate of conversion by the second quarter of the ninth century. Again, the exact numbers cannot be established, nor can it be determined what effect, if any, the expansion of Umayyad power had on conversions in the countryside. Given the Islamic background in Córdoba itself, however, the almost hysterical laments of radical Christians seem credible; they had good reason to believe that the best and brightest Christian men were being drawn to work for Muslims, to become fluent in a foreign culture, and eventually to abandon their faith altogether.

At least on the surface, converts do not appear to have been motivated by a belief in the superiority of Islamic theology. Both Latin and Arabic sources portray Christian courtiers as converting for professional reasons. Bulliet talks about conversion as a social phenomenon rather than a question of personal beliefs; the convert moved from one community to another, changing his social connections and the economic opportunities to which he had access.[33] By 850, the Islamic government officially supported the Malikite school of Islamic law, which was known for its rigidity and its aversion to innovation and reasoned debate.[34] There is evidence, though, that there was some dialogue about theology between Muslims and Christians in Córdoba; Eulogius and Albar both refer to Christians who believed that Islam and Christianity were theologically almost identical, and in some areas—particularly in beliefs about the nature of Christ—Muslims and Christians seem to have worked out compromise positions.[35]

Eulogius and Albar wrote spirited, if crude, polemic against Islam as a religion. They condemned Islam as both a social and a theological entity. Islam, they argued, encouraged moral depravity as well as corruption and exploitation in government. At the same time, they dismissed its theology as trivial and superstitious; Christianity was the only true religion, and it had absolutely nothing in common with Islam. No compromise between the two systems of belief was possible. This rigid view was echoed by the martyrs, who publicly asserted the inferiority of Islam by insulting the Prophet. At a place and time when many people were inclined to minimize the differences between Islam and Christianity, radical Christians insisted upon them.

A point of contact between Christians and Muslims that played a large role in the martyrs' movement was intermarriage between Christians and

Muslims; at least twelve of the martyrs were from religiously mixed families, and of those twelve, nine were clearly the children of mixed marriages. Islamic law prohibits marriages between Muslims and polytheists,
but it permits marriage between Muslims and *dhimmis* under certain conditions. Those conditions reflect the Muslim understanding of the husband and father as head of the family. A Muslim man may marry a *dhimmi*
woman, but a Muslim woman may only marry another Muslim. Under-
lying this rule is the assumption that the husband, as head of the family,
would be likely to convert his wife, whereas the wife, as the subordi-
nate partner, would be unable to convert her husband to her religion.[36]
Although Islamic law does not allow a husband to force his wife to convert, it does demand that the children of a mixed marriage follow the
religion of their father—that is, that they be Muslims. The martyrs from
mixed families were considered to be apostates because they rejected their
fathers' faith.

Eulogius's biographical sketches of the martyrs reveal a high level of
tension in mixed-marriage families, which emerged from the difficulties
surrounding Muslim-Christian marriages. Different standards of modesty for women prevailed among Christians and Muslims. Islamic and
Visigothic marriage laws differed; divorce, for example, though allowed
under Visigothic law in certain cases, was much easier to obtain under
Islamic law (at least for men).[37] The eighth-century jurist Malik, whose
teachings dominated theological thought in al-Andalus, believed mixed
marriages were inherently risky. A *dhimmi* wife might insist on attending church or drinking alcohol, and her husband would have no right to
stop her; she might drink while pregnant, contaminating the child in the
womb; her influence might undermine the children's faith.[38] Such differences might be less of a problem if the husband were a recent convert, one
of Bulliet's early majority, who came from a cultural background similar
to his wife's. An Iberian Christian woman married to an Arab or Berber
would face more serious cultural incompatibilities.

Eulogius does not usually specify whether the religiously mixed marriages he describes were also ethnically mixed. The family of the martyrs John, Adulphus, and Aurea is the only one he characterizes as Arab.[39]
He briefly refers to the martyr Felix, a convert from Islam to Christianity, as a member of a Berber tribe, and it is tempting to think that
he was the product of a marriage between a Muslim Berber father and
an Iberian Christian mother.[40] Evariste Lévi-Provençal theorized that the

first half of the ninth century was the period in which Arabs first began intermarrying with Iberians on a large scale,[41] but more recent research has questioned whether marriages between Arabs or Berbers and Iberians could have been as widespread as Lévi-Provençal assumed. Pierre Guichard has argued that differences between Iberian and Arab or Berber family structure were so pronounced that intermarriage was difficult and that those differences were preserved well into the tenth century.[42] According to Guichard, Arabs and Berbers in al-Andalus continued to conceive of themselves as members of tribal groups which traced their lineage exclusively through the male line and practiced strictly endogamous marriage (marriage within the kin group). Exogamous marriage, marriage outside the kin group, would bring no benefit to the family: because the tribes recognized only agnatic ties, bringing in a woman from another family would not create new relatives and allies, and even a highborn wife could not improve her husband's social standing. An Arab or Berber family, then, would oppose intermarriage with Christian Iberian women, not so much because they were Christian as because they were outside the kin group.

Genealogical sources for al-Andalus do confirm that Arabs of the period traced their kin groups primarily through the male line. In his tenth-century genealogy of the Arab families of al-Andalus (*Jamharat ansab al-Arab*), Ibn Hazm normally lists only men. When he does mention a woman it is because she is from an especially distinguished Arab family. The lineage of a man's wife or mother was not without significance, but it did not fundamentally alter the family's identity.

It is possible, though, that Guichard has exaggerated the extent to which Arab and Berber tribes remained patrilineal and endogamous. Jack Goody has suggested that even strongly patrilineal groups value connections gained through marriage ties, even if they do not recognize them for the purpose of formal genealogies; in addition, patrilineal tribal ties tend to break down in an urban environment, giving way to business relationships and ties of patronage.[43] It seems possible that as life in Córdoba came to center more and more around economic activity and the amir's court, Arab and Berber families would be willing to welcome a daughter-in-law from a wealthy or well-connected Iberian family, even though they might continue to trace their official genealogy exclusively through the male line. John, Adulphus, and Aurea may not have been the only martyrs to come from an Arab or Berber background.

Intermarriage would seem to be exactly the sort of practice that the radical Christians would condemn, but in fact they have little to say about it; Eulogius notes the cases in which a martyr came from a mixed family but passes no judgment on the situation. Those marriages placed Eulogius in a difficult position. Women who had married Muslims were, by his standards, the worst sort of traitors in one sense: they were literally sleeping with the enemy. It was usually because of the mother's influence, however, that the child became a Christian and ultimately a martyr, and thus Christian women who married Muslims could be seen as infiltrating enemy territory. Eulogius was very careful, therefore, not to criticize mixed marriages. Even though Eulogius did not address religiously mixed families as a theme, tensions in these families played an important role in the martyrdoms, as we shall see. A child of such a family might practice Christianity more or less in secret for years and then suddenly, in the 850s, decide to declare his Christianity openly and risk execution; or Muslim family members might decide with equal suddenness to accuse him before the authorities.

It is difficult to separate out the motives of individual martyrs, whose personal views of the movement are not available to us, from the motives of the radical Christian authors, who express their opinions in overwhelming detail; it would be wrong to suggest a single motive behind the movement. I would argue, though, that the movement as a whole represented a protest against and an effort to slow the process of assimilation to Arab Islamic culture that was occurring in Córdoba as a result of the Umayyad court's new vitality. This protest worked on many levels. For the radical Christian authors, it meant demonstrating the superiority and distinctiveness of Christianity as a theological system and of Latin letters. For the individual martyr, it might mean a decision to preach one's faith publicly, or to give up a good job at court to enter a monastery, or to admit to Muslim relatives that one was a Christian. The link between the authors and individual martyrs was a determination to assert Christian identity and to deny the possibility that this identity could be set aside, or made compatible with Arab Muslim culture, or kept a secret.

The radical Christian movement's immediate effect was to cause an enormous amount of trouble for Christians in Córdoba. It led to a split within the community between those who could be called pragmatic Christians—Christians involved in commerce with Muslims, or civil servants, or bishops who depended on the government for their appoint-

ments, all of whom were willing to work within the system as it existed
—and radical Christians, who perceived life under Muslim rule as intolerable. This division led to upheaval and chaos within the Cordovan
Christian community, and particularly within the church hierarchy. The
movement also caused friction between Christians and Muslims. The
Islamic government treated the martyrs' movement as it would any form
of serious disobedience on the part of a subject group: by executing or
otherwise making examples of the guilty, putting pressure on community
leaders, and generally making life as inconvenient as possible for all Christians. In the end, not surprisingly, the process of assimilation continued,
and the radical Christian movement had little long-term effect. What is
important about the radical Christians, though, is not their ultimate fail-
ure but that their movement highlights the processes of conversion and
assimilation within an Islamic society. It is easy to discuss those processes
in a detached and disinterested manner from the distance of time, but the
radical Christian movement in Córdoba forces us to see the personal costs
that such profound social changes could exact on contemporaries.

2

The Martyrs' Movement

Rather than discussing each martyr in chronological order, which has been done elsewhere,[1] this chapter will treat the martyrs thematically, by first examining the origins of the movement; then looking at specific martyrs as examples, with attention to the distinction between those executed as non-Muslims who insulted the Prophet and those convicted of apostasy from Islam; and finally by analyzing the Islamic government's reactions to these events.

Eulogius refers to two early martyrs, the brothers Adulphus and John, who were executed in the early 820s, some thirty years before the main group of Cordovan martyrs.[2] Eulogius's teacher Abbot Speraindeo wrote a biography of the brothers which has not survived, so that we cannot determine the circumstances of their deaths or know whether Adulphus and John served as models for the martyrs of the 850s. If later Christians did think of them as models, then the martyrs' movement can be said to have begun with an Arab family.

Eulogius describes the death of Adulphus and John's sister Aurea, who was executed in 856.[3] Aurea and her mother, Artemia, were Christian nuns but came from what Eulogius characterizes as a noble Arab family. Among their relatives was Ahmad ibn Ziyad, the *qadi* of Córdoba between 854 and 864, and this same family produced two other *qadi*s as well.[4] Aurea's Arab Muslim relatives, who lived in Seville rather than Córdoba, had overlooked her Christianity for most of her adult life. In the tense,

anti-Christian atmosphere generated by the martyrs' movement, however, they felt that they must force Aurea to profess Islam. When she refused to do so, she was executed as an apostate. The years leading up to the
execution of John and Adulphus in the 820s were similarly a time of tension between Christians and Muslims and of Christian protests against the
government. Those protests targeted, among other grievances, the amir's
appointment of a Christian named Rabia, a man regarded as dishonest
and unscrupulous by Christians and Muslims alike, as *qumis* (a title deriv-
ing from the Latin *comes,* or count), the official in charge of the Christian
community and responsible for collecting its taxes.[5]

A reasonable supposition would be that this was a predominantly Arab
family which by the 820s had intermarried with Iberian Christian women
who raised some of their children as Christians; that the family normally
allowed Christian members to go their own way but pressured them to
acknowledge Islam during times of anti-Christian tensions; and that during such times the family might seek the execution of extraordinarily
defiant Christian kinsmen as apostates. If John and Adulphus were in fact
models for the later martyrs, then the martyrs' movement had its origins
in the issue of apostasy and the problems of religiously mixed families.

Whatever the impact of earlier examples, the martyrdoms of the 850s
developed more or less spontaneously out of confrontations in the streets.
The first person to be executed was a priest named Perfectus, who according to Eulogius was a student of Scripture and also fluent in Arabic.[6]
One day while running errands he was stopped by a group of Muslims
who ordered him to state his beliefs about Christ and Muhammad. He replied (in Arabic) that he believed in Christ's divinity but preferred not to
say anything about their Prophet unless they were willing to make a pact
of friendship. The Muslims agreed to the pact, at which point Perfectus
launched into an attack against Muhammad. Muhammad, he said, taught
false doctrine; he was seduced by demonic images and led his followers to
perdition; he committed adultery with Zaynab, wife of his follower Zayd,
"blinded by her beauty, carrying her off in accordance with his barbaric
law, like a horse or mule which has no understanding." Perfectus finished
with a catalog of the "foulness and lust" which Muhammad's law dictated.

After this less than diplomatic outburst, Perfectus returned to his errands. He had made enemies, however, and when those same Muslims
next saw him on the street, they called out, "Here is the one who spoke
abusively of the prophet." An angry crowd surrounded Perfectus and

carried him to the court of the *qadi,* who sentenced him to death. Perfectus at first denied the charges against him out of fear but soon changed his mind, realizing that he would be executed anyway. He was imprisoned for several months, then beheaded; according to Eulogius, he made another speech condemning Muhammad shortly before his execution.

What happened to Perfectus was not a purely spontaneous event. He was a priest at the basilica of St. Acisclus. The basilicas in Córdoba were centers of radical Christian education; Eulogius reports that the martyr Sisenandus had come to Córdoba specifically to study at St. Acisclus, which became the burial place of several martyrs.[7] What he said about Muhammad followed the standard line of the antiassimilationist Christians in Córdoba, and the remark about Muhammad's adultery with Zaynab came directly from a Christian biography of the Prophet which Eulogius was circulating in the early 850s.[8] Perfectus did not think up these criticisms of Muhammad on the spot; he was well rehearsed. It is also unlikely that the Muslims he spoke with were simply accosting Christians randomly and asking their views on Christ and Muhammad. They were probably familiar with the views of radical Christians and had identified Perfectus as part of that group. He said what they expected to hear.

Although Perfectus spoke harshly, he was not actively seeking martyrdom; he tried to protect himself by extracting a promise of friendship from his listeners. He made his denunciation of Muhammad in front of the *qadi* only after he had already been sentenced and had nothing more to lose. Perfectus was inviting danger by speaking out as he did, but his martyrdom was in some sense an accident.

The next incident that Eulogius and Albar record is the beating of a Christian merchant named John, which occurred almost a year after Perfectus's death.[9] A group of Muslim merchants in the marketplace began harassing John because of his habit of swearing by the Prophet: "You often take our prophet's name in vain, thinking little of him, and to people who do not know you are a Christian you often confirm your lies [about your merchandise] with oaths of our religion, even though you believe them to be false." As the merchants continued to hurl accusations, John lost his temper and yelled, "God damn anyone who wants to use your prophet's name." A crowd attacked John and dragged him to the *qadi,* who ordered that he be beaten. Next he was led in chains to each church in Córdoba, followed by a crier who informed onlookers that "he who insults the Prophet of God must suffer like this." John was then sent to prison, where Eulogius met him later that year during his own incarceration. His ultimate fate is unknown, but neither Eulogius nor Albar reports his execution. Most likely the *qadi* did not consider his words to merit the death penalty because strictly speaking his outburst was directed at Muslims in the crowd, not at Muhammad himself.

The incident involving John confirms that the atmosphere in Córdoba was tense even before the first voluntary martyr came forward. The Muslims who attacked John, like those who accosted Perfectus, were looking for a fight. Albar reports that it was not unusual for Christians in Córdoba to pass as Muslims[10] so that what John was doing, letting people think he was Muslim and swearing by Muhammad, was probably nothing out of the ordinary. On that particular day, though, Muslims took offense. The experiences of Perfectus and John also show that tensions between Muslims and Christians were already focused on Christian opinion about Muhammad.

John's predicament, even more than Perfectus's, was unplanned. He does not appear to have had any intention of insulting Muhammad, and what happened to him was the result of a crowd's anger escalating out of control. Both incidents captured the imaginations of some Cordovan Christians, however. Aurelius, who was executed in 852, saw John led through the streets in chains and was moved by his courage in the face of suffering; Aurelius said that his own craving for an ascetic way of life, and eventually for martyrdom, began at that moment.[11] At some point, certain radical Christians made the mental leap from admiring John's or Perfectus's courage to placing themselves intentionally in the same position.

The first person deliberately to seek execution was Isaac, a Christian who at one time had been a civil servant in the Islamic government.[12] Isaac's parents, Eulogius writes, were Cordovan citizens, of the nobility, and rich. Albar and Eulogius refer to several people as "noble" or "citizens," but the sources do not tell us whether these terms reflect privileges still enjoyed under Islamic rule or the memory of privileges enjoyed by the family in Visigothic times. Isaac was well-trained in Arabic, and when still a young man he came to occupy the post of *exceptor rei publicae*. The exact nature of that office is a subject of debate, but it is certain that the *exceptor* was among the most important Christian officials and probable that he was in charge of collecting taxes; the official may be the same one identified in Arabic as *qumis*.[13]

Wealthy, young, and successful, Isaac abruptly left office and entered a monastery: as Eulogius puts it, "unexpectedly, burning with spiritual fire and desiring a monastic life, he traveled to [the monastery of] Tabanos." After three years in the monastery, he returned to the city and went to the *qadi*'s court. Pretending that he wished to convert, he asked the *qadi* to tell him about Islam. When the *qadi* began to explain Islamic doctrine, Isaac interrupted him and, in Arabic, called Muhammad a liar, saying he was filled with the devil and would lead his followers to eternal damnation. He begged the *qadi* to abandon "the excrescence of this pestiferous doctrine" and become a Christian. The *qadi* was so overcome by what he heard that he burst into tears and slapped Isaac. Rebuked by the men around him for losing his temper, he then suggested that Isaac must be insane or drunk and thus unable to appreciate the seriousness of his words. When Isaac insisted that he was in his right mind, the *qadi* ordered him jailed and sent word of the incident to the amir. The amir had Isaac beheaded and published an edict to the effect that any Christian insulting the Prophet would meet a similar fate.

Muslim officials took Isaac's case very seriously. Unlike Perfectus, who was put in jail to be dealt with more conveniently at a later date, Isaac was immediately brought to the amir's attention, and the government felt it necessary to issue a decree emphasizing the legal consequences of insulting the Prophet. From the government's point of view, Isaac's actions were much more threatening than those of a radical Christian priest like Perfectus, from whom one would expect strange behavior. Isaac had been a government official, a Christian but nevertheless a colleague. He had been out of office for only three years before his execution and so probably still had friends in the government. The *qadi*, Said ibn Sulayman, had taken office only three years earlier, in 848.[14] He may have been so shocked by Isaac's speech because he had known Isaac at court.

Eulogius devotes considerable space to Isaac's story, in part because Isaac was the first truly voluntary martyr (at least of the 850s). But Isaac was also an important symbol for radical Christians in that his conversion to monastic life represented a decisive break with his past. Radical Christians in Córdoba and Christian officials appointed by the Islamic government, especially those with the power to collect taxes, were generally implacable enemies. Christians like Eulogius viewed such officials as greedy, lustful, gluttonous, and in general hopelessly corrupted by contact with Muslims, while Christian officials were extremely hostile to the beliefs and actions of radical Christians, whom they viewed as fanatics and troublemakers.[15] Isaac underwent a conversion from his life as tax collector to the monastic life of Tabanos. Tabanos was a center of radical Christian thought—at least ten of the martyrs over the next decade were associated with Tabanos, and it was also known for the unusually strict ascetic observances of its monks and nuns.[16] Isaac's move from the palace to Tabanos and his subsequent martyrdom suggested that the trend toward assimilation to Islam could be reversed and that radical Christian ideals could turn assimilated Christians in government against their masters. This new possibility was welcomed by Christians like Eulogius but represented a potentially serious problem for the Muslim authorities.

The only other government official to be martyred was Argimirus, who died in June 856.[17] Argimirus held the office of *censor*, the judge who presided over the legal affairs of the Christian community.[18] After retiring from that position, he entered a monastery. Certain Muslims complained to the *qadi* that he had made derogatory remarks about the Prophet. Argimirus did not deny the charges and was executed.

Isaac and Argimirus were the only former government officials to be executed, but in one sense they were typical of many of the martyrs: they were connected with a monastery. Eulogius writes that he had originally expected to address his works exclusively to the monasteries.[19] The martyrs in fact proved to be a more diverse group than Eulogius had anticipated, but the movement continued to draw heavily on the monastic population—twenty-one of the martyrs are specifically identified by Eulogius as monks or nuns—and many others influenced by the ascetic practices typical of Cordovan monasticism.

The Cordovan monasteries were ideal breeding grounds for radical thought. They were isolated; all of those mentioned by Eulogius were outside the walls of Córdoba, sometimes by a distance of several miles.[20] They were close-knit communities, often based on blood ties—Tabanos, for example, was founded by Elizabeth, her husband, Jeremiah, and their extended family. Later Elizabeth's brother Martin became abbot.[21] They apparently were also small communities. In 852 a monk from Jerusalem visited Córdoba and told Eulogius that there were more than five hundred monks at his monastery, Mar Sabas; in his account of that conversation, Eulogius emphasizes that he heard this number from George's own mouth, as though he does not expect his readers to believe it.[22]

It is not clear what rule the Cordovan houses followed, although they were certainly not Benedictine communities.[23] What is clear, however, is that strict asceticism and grave anxieties about salvation were integral parts of Cordovan monastic life. This ascetic emphasis is illustrated by Eulogius's accounts of the martyrs Habentius and Columba.[24] Habentius was executed for denouncing Muhammad in June 851, in the company of five other men (one priest and four monks); one of the men in this group was Jeremiah, the cofounder of Tabanos. Habentius lived apart from his fellow monks at St. Christopher's monastery: "There [at the monastery] he was dead to the world and endured a very strict rule for Christ's sake. He willingly had himself shut away in a cell; from within, surrounded by high walls and held fast with iron bonds against his flesh, he showed himself through breaches in the wall to visitors."

Columba was a nun at Tabanos and was the sister of Elizabeth and Martin. She, like Habentius, lived in a cell apart from the community and engaged in strict asceticism, including vigils, fasts, extended periods of prayer, and weeping so severe that tears soaked the mat of her cell. She worried constantly that these disciplines would not be enough to ensure her salvation:

> The devil wore her out with anxieties, caused her to feel disgust, showed her images of men and of food and harassed her with various fantasies. She mourned greatly because of these troubles, terribly afraid lest by a deadly slip on her part she be separated from the companionship of her husband, for whom she claimed to be burning inside with such a great fire of love, that she felt wounded in her mind with desire for him, as though by a scar of cut flesh; nor would she believe she was saved until she caught sight of him in heaven.

In September 853, Columba went before the *qadi* denouncing the Prophet and was subsequently beheaded.

The Cordovan monasteries may have been influenced by North African and Middle Eastern practices. In the 550s and 560s Christian ascetics fled to southern Spain from North Africa because they disagreed with the theological positions Emperor Justinian tried to impose on them.[25] During the Muslim period there was easy communication between al-Andalus and the Middle East, as is witnessed by George's presence in Córdoba in 852. The practices of Cordovan ascetics like Habentius and Columba were similar to those followed at George's monastery of Mar Sabas, where monks lived as semianchorites, spending most of their time engaged in ascetic practices in individual cells but still meeting for communal services and meals.[26]

Whatever the origins of their practices, the Cordovan monasteries produced men and women who were deeply committed to asceticism, fearful about their salvation, and ready to do whatever was necessary to affirm their Christian beliefs and discredit Islam. These were the people Eulogius called spiritual athletes, who came out of their cells in the countryside around Córdoba to protest the execution of Perfectus.[27] Even the martyrs who were not monks or nuns often had some connections with the monasteries and practiced similar disciplines in their own homes. Eulogius's initial prediction that the martyrs would come out of the monasteries was in a sense correct; the movement was deeply infused with Cordovan monasticism's asceticism and its anxiety about salvation.

The monastic life and asceticism were ideals uniting many of the martyrs; monks and nuns formed the largest subgroup within the martyrs' movement. The second most important subgroup were the apostates — those who had either practiced Islam at one time or who had Muslim fathers and were therefore legally classified as Muslims. Their crime was professing Christianity; they were executed as lapsed Muslims rather than as *dhimmi*s insulting the Prophet, and the pattern of their arrest and execution was somewhat different from that of the other martyrs. The fact that at least a dozen of the martyrs fit into this category of apostates from mixed families shows that the martyrs' movement cannot be understood solely as a dispute between Muslim rulers and Christian fanatics in the monasteries. The conflict was also deeply embedded in Cordovan family life.

The first apostates whom Eulogius discusses in detail were the sisters Nunilo and Alodia, who died in October 851.[28] They were executed in Bosca, not Córdoba, but Eulogius understood them to be linked to the Cordovan movement. Nunilo and Alodia were the daughters of a Christian mother and a Muslim father who had allowed his wife to raise the girls as Christians. When he died, however, the mother married another Muslim who was not so broad-minded. To avoid friction with their stepfather, the sisters were sent to live with a Christian maternal aunt. Devoting themselves to ascetic practices, they soon became known in the area for their piety — too well-known, apparently, because eventually a family enemy went to the local authorities and identified the sisters as apostates.

The Muslim prefect promised the sisters many rewards, including help in making advantageous marriages, if they would renounce their Christianity; he promised them torture and death if they would not. They were placed in the custody of a Muslim woman for instruction in the faith. When they continued to claim that they were Christians, they were beheaded in the town square.

Nunilo and Alodia's story shows a pattern similar to those of other apostates. They were not executed for denouncing Muhammad but for practicing Christianity. As was true of several other apostates, their martyrdom was only partially voluntary; although they had engaged in risky behavior, they did not come before the authorities willingly but were informed against by a neighbor. Their case, more than Isaac's, points in obvious ways to personal rather than ideological conflicts—among neighbors, between husband and wife, between daughter and stepfather, between Christians and Muslims in the same family.

The apostate to receive the most attention from Eulogius was Flora, who with her companion Maria was executed in November 851.[29] Eulogius claims to have known Flora since she was a child and gives a detailed account of her life. Her mother was a "noble" Christian woman and her father a Muslim, originally from Seville. Her father died when Flora was a young child, and from that point on her mother raised Flora and her sister as Christians. Flora could not practice her faith openly, however, because her brother was a devout Muslim. This need for secrecy disturbed her, and she thought often of Matthew 10:32–33, "Whoever acknowledges me before men, I will acknowledge before my father in heaven, and whoever denies me before men, I will deny before my father in heaven." (Eulogius quotes these verses frequently in relation to secret Christians who decided to come forward.)

One day she and her sister ran away from home and went into hiding with Christians. Their brother was beside himself with anger; he used his influence with the authorities to disrupt monasteries, where he suspected that his sisters were hiding, and to have several priests jailed. When Flora heard about his actions she returned home to confront him, saying that she was a Christian and that he could do nothing to change her mind. He dragged Flora to the *qadi* and accused her of apostasy, testifying that she had once been a good Muslim but that Christians had seduced her away from Islam "by some smooth talk." Flora replied that she had always known Christ in her heart and had never been a Muslim (and, by implication, was not an apostate). The *qadi* had her beaten until the bone at the base of her neck was laid bare, then sent her home with her brother. A few nights later she ran away again and went into hiding with her sister in Martos, where she remained for six years.[30] She finally returned to Córdoba and declared her Christianity before the *qadi,* who promptly arrested her.

Flora was arrested along with her companion Maria. Maria's case was unusual in that her father was a Christian and her mother a Muslim who converted to Christianity. Because such a marriage was prohibited by Islamic law and would have constituted an act of apostasy on the mother's part even if she had not formally converted, the couple lost all their property. When their mother died, Maria and her brother Walabonsus were sent to monastic communities to be cared for. Walabonsus was martyred in June 851.[31] He later appeared in a vision to one of the nuns in Maria's community and announced that Maria would soon join him. Shortly thereafter, she walked into Córdoba and at the church of St. Acisclus met Flora. The two went together to the *qadi*'s court, where they affirmed their faith in Christ and called Muhammad an adulterer, a magician, and a criminal. Both were arrested.

Flora and Maria were kept in prison for several weeks while the authorities tried to convince them to recant their statements. Their arrest, in fact, touched off the government's first large-scale reaction to the martyrs' movement. The government's tactics centered on pressuring clergy, whom officials believed (correctly) were connected with the unrest. Several clergy were jailed during Flora and Maria's imprisonment, including Eulogius and Saul, the bishop of Córdoba.[32] These arrests, according to Paul Albar, were instigated by Reccafred, the archbishop of Seville, whom Albar and Eulogius both judged to be a puppet of the Muslims.[33] The government probably hoped that arrests of dissident clergy would demoralize radical Christians in general and perhaps persuade Flora and Maria to cooperate. At the same time, the *qadi* put pressure on the two women directly, threatening to sell them into prostitution and giving them ample time in jail to reflect on their situation.[34]

Muslim officials would probably not have gone to so much trouble if only Maria had been arrested. Maria's precise legal status is unclear. Islamic law generally assumes that the father determines his child's religion, which would place Maria in the category of a Christian denouncing Muhammad; a few legal authorities, however, hold that if either parent is

Muslim the child must be a Muslim, which would make Maria an apostate.[35] She was in any event from a family that was impoverished, discredited, and in which all the men we know of were Christians — which from the Muslim point of view defined the family as Christian. Flora, however, was from a family in which the men we know about were Muslims and which was important enough that the government had thoroughly disrupted the Christian community when Flora disappeared six years earlier. The fact that she was from a good family and was clearly an apostate, the first the Cordovan authorities had encountered (at least in the 850s), must have been troubling because it suggested that radical Christian ideas were not confined to the monasteries and could directly affect Muslims' lives. In addition, Flora and Maria were the first women confessors to come forward in Córdoba, which raised difficult questions for the authorities. Some legal experts held that women apostates should be beaten rather than executed, a course of action the qadi had followed six years earlier in Flora's case;[36] now, however, Flora's actions seemed to demand the death penalty.

The significance of Flora's adherence to Christianity was not lost on Eulogius. He was in prison at the same time as Flora and Maria, having been picked up in the government's sweep of Christian clergy, and while incarcerated he wrote the Documentum martyriale to encourage Maria and Flora in their resolve to be martyred. The Documentum was intended to counteract the pressure the government was exerting on the two women and was also a reply to members of the Christian community who felt that Flora and Maria had gone too far and believed they should be dissuaded from martyrdom.[37] In the Documentum, Eulogius reminds the confessors of the rewards they will receive after death. He particularly emphasizes that as virgin martyrs they will be brides of Christ: "This way [martyrdom] will more easily and quickly bring you to your husband's chamber."[38] He also commends their struggle as doubly significant because it forced them to overcome their natural weakness as women.[39] In his preoccupation with virginity and feminine weakness and in his liberal use of bridal imagery, Eulogius in the Documentum sounds very much like Jerome, whom he at one point quotes directly.[40]

Although ostensibly written for both women, the Documentum was aimed primarily at Flora, whose religious background and social status made her martyrdom an important symbol. Eulogius writes to Flora that the martyrs will become known the world over because of her and comments on her special status as the daughter of a Muslim father: "You, created out of a wolfish union and born by your gentle mother, have grown like a rose among brambles." [41] Near the end of the *Documentum*, Eulogius makes much of his relationship with Flora. He reminds Flora of how he came to visit her after she had been beaten, how he saw the skin torn away from the neck, the gaping wound, "and with a soft hand I stroked it, because I did not think such wounds should be caressed with kisses." [42] He is nearly a father to her, he says. Drawing on Psalm 44, he urges her to forget about her own family and her father's home. [43] Eulogius, apparently, will be her new father, her Christian father. Eulogius's tone when he addresses women is very similar to Jerome's: simultaneously seductive, fatherly, and badgering. Just as Eulogius hoped, Flora and Maria refused to recant their statements and were executed.

In July 852 a group of four relatives were put to death for apostasy —Aurelius, his wife, Sabigotho, Aurelius's relative Felix, and his wife, Liliosa. [44] These four displayed a confusing array of religious affiliations.

Aurelius came from a rich family; his father was a Muslim, his mother a Christian, and after Aurelius was orphaned at a young age he was raised by a Christian paternal aunt. When he reached adolescence, his Muslim relatives decided that he should study Arabic letters and presumably that he should practice Islam. He remained an ardent Christian, but now that his Muslim relatives had taken notice of him he had to keep his beliefs secret.

Aurelius married Nathalia, both of whose parents were Muslims. [45] Her mother married a second time, however, to a man who was secretly a Christian. He converted both mother and daughter, and Nathalia was baptized and given the name Sabigotho—a Visigothic name, which the family may have favored as evoking a Christian era. Because of the Muslim background of their families, neither Sabigotho nor Aurelius could live openly as Christians without risking charges of apostasy, but the couple continued to practice their faith in secret. One day Aurelius witnessed the beating of the merchant John in the town square. He was moved by John's suffering and his courage and resolved to lead a more pious life. From that day on, Aurelius and Sabigotho lived a more openly Christian and ascetic life; they were celibate, fasted and prayed, spent time at the monastery of Tabanos, and visited Eulogius, Flora, and Maria in prison. Soon they were considering seeking martyrdom themselves.

Aurelius's relative Felix and Felix's wife, Liliosa, were contemplating martyrdom at the same time. Felix came from a Christian family and had converted to Islam, then back to Christianity. Because of his conversion to Islam, he had to practice Christianity in secret to avoid charges of apostasy. Liliosa was also a secret Christian.

At Tabanos the four relatives met George, the most exotic of the martyrs. George was born in Bethlehem and had spent the last twenty-seven years as a monk at Mar Sabas near Jerusalem. There he had followed a strict ascetic regimen. He was a student of languages and was fluent in Greek, Latin, and Arabic. While in North Africa to collect a donation for his monastery, he heard that the church in Spain was oppressed and decided to cross over to investigate. Once in Córdoba he gravitated to Tabanos, probably hearing of its reputation for asceticism, and there he met Sabigotho. The next day he accompanied Sabigotho into Córdoba and asked Aurelius, Felix, and Liliosa if he could be martyred with them.

The goal of the four secret Christians was to be arrested for apostasy. They decided that their aim could be accomplished most efficiently if the women went to a Christian church with their faces uncovered; appearing without veils would allow them to be recognized and at the same time demonstrate that they did not consider themselves to be Muslims. On their way home they ran into an official who recognized them. The official went immediately to Felix and Aurelius and asked them to explain why their wives were seen coming out of a church. The men replied that they were all Christians. Soon afterward both couples were arrested. No one wanted to arrest George because he was a foreigner and had done nothing wrong, so he quickly made an insulting remark about Muhammad. The *qadi* ordered all five to be executed.

Aurelius's family background illustrates themes that recur in Eulogius's biographical sketches of the martyrs. One is that religiously mixed families did not operate by a consistent set of rules governing the religious affiliation of members. Islamic law provides such rules, but families enforced them only sporadically; thus Aurelius came under pressure to practice Islam only as an adolescent, although the law identified him as a Muslim from birth. The same inconsistency can be seen in Nunilo and Alodia's family, in which father and stepfather had very different ideas of how the girls should be raised. This lack of a clear policy contributed to the confusion and hostility within mixed families. It also supports the theory that religiously mixed marriages had only recently become common—either because Berber and Arab families were now intermarrying with Iberians, or because the early majority phenomenon meant that many of the marriageable men in a Christian woman's social set were now converting to Islam, or both—and that people were not yet sure of the ground rules. The behavior of Aurelius's family also confirms Albar and Eulogius's observation that young men were in particular danger of being drawn into Islamic culture. Muslims in this family apparently tolerated Christianity among women and children but considered it inappropriate for a young man ready to seek his place in the world.

In March 857, a priest named Rudericus was executed as an apostate.[46] Rudericus had two brothers, one a Christian and one a convert to Islam; the two fought constantly. One night when Rudericus tried to intervene during one of their battles, they both turned on him and beat him insensible. The Muslim brother put the unconscious Rudericus on a stretcher and had him carried from quarter to quarter, proclaiming that his brother the priest had embraced Islam and wanted everyone to know of his conversion in case he should die from his injuries. When Rudericus recovered and learned what his brother had done, he fled Córdoba; for him to appear publicly in his priest's robes could now be construed as an act of apostasy. After a few days Rudericus grew tired of hiding and returned to Córdoba, apparently still wearing clerical robes. He had the misfortune to run into his Muslim brother on the street; the brother had him arrested and brought before the *qadi* as an apostate. Rudericus denied the charges, maintaining that he had never converted to Islam and thus could not be an apostate. The *qadi* believed the brother, however, and told Rudericus that he could either acknowledge that he was a Muslim or die. Rudericus chose execution.

The level of disharmony in Rudericus's religiously mixed family is striking. When he took on the thankless role of peacemaker, Rudericus became the object of the intense hostility his brothers felt for each other, a hostility caused, or at least expressed, by their religious differences. A similar hostility existed in Flora's family; her brother accused her publicly of apostasy, knowing that she could be executed or at least severely punished. Hatred between relatives in mixed families was one of the engines that powered the martyrs' movement.

Rudericus and his companion Salomon were the last martyrs about whom Eulogius wrote. In 859 Eulogius himself was executed, along with a young girl named Leocritja, who was convicted of apostasy.

Albar describes the death of Eulogius and Leocritja in his biography of Eulogius.[47] Leocritja was from a "noble" Muslim family; echoing Eulogius's words about Flora, Albar writes that she was "born out of the filth of the gentiles and brought forth from the flesh of wolves." Leocritja's parents were both Muslims, but a relative named Litiosa, a Christian nun, had the girl baptized in secret. As a child Leocritja was a secret Christian. She became more openly devout and ascetic as she grew older, much to her parents' distress; when they could not persuade her to forgo her practices, they resorted to beating her. Fearing that she could not be a good Christian unless she expressed her beliefs more openly, she asked advice from Eulogius, who was "already renowned for such works." Eulogius "recognized his accustomed duty" and advised her to leave home. Leocritja, like Flora, offered Eulogius an opportunity he could not refuse: the prospect of a young girl from a respected and predominantly Muslim family publicly embracing Christianity. Leocritja pretended for a time to go along with her parents' wishes. She abandoned her ascetic practices and adorned herself with jewels and thus diverted suspicion from herself. One day she dressed in her best clothes and said she was going to a relative's wedding. Instead she went to the home of Eulogius and his sister Anulo, who hid her with Christian friends. Once in hiding, she returned to her practices of fasting, keeping vigils, and wearing a hair shirt.

Leocritja's parents were deeply upset when they discovered she was missing. They prevailed upon the qadi to have priests and various other Christians jailed, hoping to pressure the community into returning their daughter. One night Leocritja came to visit Eulogius and Anulo; someone had informed the authorities that she would be there, and the house was soon surrounded by soldiers. Eulogius and Leocritja were arrested.

Eulogius had been arrested before on the basis of vague, or not so vague, suspicions that he had encouraged the martyrdoms. This time, however, he had been caught harboring a runaway girl from an important Muslim family and encouraging her to apostasize. He was questioned by the amir's counselors. One of these was, according to Albar, very well-known to Eulogius and offered to help him escape. Eulogius refused the offer, and he and Leocritja were executed shortly thereafter.

Cases like those of Leocritja and the other apostates offer fascinating, if limited, glimpses of Cordovan family life. They suggest that intermarriage between Christian and Muslim families was fairly common; that the children of such marriages were not necessarily raised as Muslims, despite Islamic law; that some family members might convert to Islam while others (typically women) remained Christian; and that any of these situations could generate tremendous tensions within the family.

The government correctly perceived the confessors' actions as a challenge to Islamic authority and used various tactics to discourage further martyrdoms. One such tactic was the arrest of clergymen, which was intended to destroy morale among radical Christians by incarcerating clergy who supported the martyrdoms. Eulogius maintained that the bishops, priests, abbots, and deacons who were arrested had no influence over the martyrs and that the Muslims were merely "imputing to our instigation and ascribing to our planning whatever the illustrious ones did because of divine will,"[48] but this statement seems disingenuous given his personal involvement with several of the martyrs and the support monastic institutions gave to the movement. The government also hoped to control radical Christians by putting pressure on prominent members of their community. Traditional Islamic governments coped with social problems through pressure on group leaders; if there was a problem involving a certain quarter of the city or a certain religious group, leading citizens of that community were expected to solve it.[49] Albar and Eulogius were bitter that Archbishop Reccafred of Seville ordered the arrest of clergymen; but the government's policy of pressuring community leaders and the amir's control of episcopal appointments probably gave Reccafred little choice in the matter. Pressure from the government affected lay leaders as well as clergy so that by the time of Abd al-Rahman's death in September 852, no "noble laymen" dared to approach the palace gates for fear of being arrested.[50]

The extent of the amir's influence over church affairs was demonstrated in 852, when Abd al-Rahman called a council of bishops and metropolitans to address the problem of the martyrdoms.[51] Attending the council as the amir's representative was a Christian official whom Eulogius (who was also present) identified as the *exceptor rei publicae,* the same post Isaac once occupied. This official apparently insulted Eulogius at the council, and Eulogius devotes considerable space to denouncing him as an embodiment of greed, cruelty, and injustice. The *exceptor* ordered that the martyrs be anathematized, and in response the council issued an ambiguous decree about the martyrdoms; according to Eulogius, it appeared superficially to condemn the martyrdoms, but a closer reading reveals that it did not in fact do so. Eulogius adds that he does not approve of such dissimulation, but on the other hand he appears satisfied that the council did not condemn the martyrs. The *exceptor* was also apparently satisfied with the decree. The bishops seem to have issued a cautiously ambiguous statement from which each side could draw its own conclusions.

The government also sought to punish the entire Christian community for the martyrs' actions by enforcing rules pertaining to the *dhimma* more strictly than was usual and in some cases by going beyond those rules. When Muhammad I became amir after the death of Abd al-Rahman, he dismissed all of the Christian officials at the palace and ordered the destruction of all recently constructed churches and monasteries and all additions to older churches which had been put in place since the Muslim invasion of 711. Technically, the amir was only enforcing the letter of Islamic law; the law prohibits *dhimmis* from holding positions of authority over Muslims and allows them to maintain previously established churches and synagogues but not to improve them or construct new ones. Before the martyrdoms began, however, the Cordovan government, like other Islamic governments, had consistently used *dhimmis* as civil servants. Muhammad I's dismissal of Christians, but not Jews, shows that his real interest was retaliation for the martyrdoms rather than religious purity at court.[52] Similarly, the ban against new churches and monasteries had not been enforced consistently before the martyrdoms; Tabanos, for example, was recently founded (its founders were alive in the 850s), but it was not targeted for destruction until after it became associated with the martyrs. Some of Muhammad I's measures went beyond strict observance of the *dhimma*. He imposed new taxes on Christians, apparently in addition to the normal poll tax, and hired other Christians to collect it, which effectively divided the Christian community. He deprived Christians who had served in the army of their military pensions. Eulogius also claims that the amir considered having all Christian men put to death and all Christian women sold into slavery but that his advisers dissuaded him from this course.[53]

Muslim harassment of *dhimmis* was not confined to ninth-century Córdoba. In *A Mediterranean Society,* S. D. Goitein describes the case of a twelfth-century Saljuq sultan of Baghdad who wished to collect some extraordinary funds from *dhimmi* communities. He announced that the rule requiring *dhimmis* to wear distinctive dress would now be enforced and issued complex regulations regarding that dress: non-Muslim women, for example, would wear one black shoe and one red and a bell on their shoes or neck. Faced with a choice between abiding by these elaborate rules or giving a cash settlement, the *dhimmi*s elected to pay what was asked.[54] The reality for *dhimmi*s was that the Muslim ruler had great power over them; Islamic law technically limited the government's ability to harm non-Muslims, but in practice the ruler decided when and how harshly laws discriminating against Jews and Christians would be enforced. It seems farfetched that Muhammad I would seriously consider mass executions of Christians, but he was clearly prepared to make life as unpleasant for them as possible. In effect, he gave Christians a choice: stop the martyrdoms or face harassment, loss of jobs, and financial hardship.

Christians responded to the government's pressures in various ways. Some who were in danger of arrest went into hiding. Eulogius reports that he and some other wanted Christians changed residences frequently and used disguises.[55] Bishop Saul fled Córdoba in 853.[56] Others pretended not to be Christian or converted to Islam outright; the *exceptor*, for example, was able to remain in government service by converting.[57] Still others remained Christian but became vehement opponents of the martyrs' movement, which they correctly saw as the source of their current difficulties: "But when the growing divine fire inflamed many and led crowds of the faithful to go down to the square and denounce the enemy of the church with the same confession of faith that Isaac had made, soon everyone, frightened by the rage of the savage tyrant, with amazing fickleness changed their minds; they disparaged and cursed the martyrs, and declared that both the martyrs themselves and their supporters were authors of a great crime."[58] Sometime before 854, a group of Christian notables—bishops, abbots, priests, nobles, and magnates—went before the *qadi* and publicly denounced the martyrs as heretics.[59] As the decade of the 850s unfolded, pressure from the government took an increasing toll on the Christian community, which tended to polarize between radical and more moderate Christians.

There are isolated reports of voluntary martyrdoms in al-Andalus after Eulogius's death.[60] It is possible that there were additional, unrecorded martyrdoms; but the phenomenon of large groups of Christians seeking death seems to have been confined to the 850s. Although chance and circumstances played a role in deciding who would become a martyr, there is a definite shape to the chronology of the movement. It began more or less spontaneously, with the explosion of Muslim anger against Perfectus. Soon, though, a pattern of voluntary martyrdom was established. During the movement's first months, most of the martyrs were monks. By late in 851, however, Christians from mixed families began to come forward, and many of them were women. That the participants were so diverse and that so many of the martyrs came from partially Muslim families indicate that the movement was not a simple attack against Islam from outside. It was the very closeness of Christians and Muslims and the complex and ambivalent nature of their relationships that produced the martyrdoms.

3

Eulogius and Albar: The Martyrs and the Polemic Against Islam

I have argued that Eulogius and Albar accurately presented in their works the basic events of the martyrs' movement. Their interpretation of those events was, however, influenced by their own specific agenda, which was to prove that those who died were true martyrs; to demonstrate that Islam was an entirely evil and unacceptable system of belief; and to condemn Christians who favored accommodation with their Muslim rulers. Their writings suggest that these views emerged out of a mixture of ideological fanaticism and personal resentments.

The bases for the latter are hinted at in the sources, although it is difficult to piece together a full biographical picture of either Eulogius or Albar. Our main source of biographical information about Eulogius is Albar's *Vita Eulogii*. The *Vita* describes in detail the events leading up to Eulogius's execution. Beyond that particular episode, however, Albar was less interested in establishing a narrative of Eulogius's life than in emphasizing Eulogius's virtues and his connections with the martyrs' movement. We are told that Eulogius was a person of substance who came from a "noble senatorial family."[1] He was respected even at the Islamic court, where one of the amir's counselors commended his virtuous way of life and offered him a means to escape execution.[2] Albar, like Eulogius, was eager to establish that those involved in the martyrs' movement were wellborn and educated. They may have been responding to allegations by Muslims (and probably some Christians) that the movement was popular only among the uneducated. According to Eulogius, a counselor to Muhammad I told the amir that no one who was *"urbanus"* was involved, that is, no one who understood the niceties of civilized, urban life or the rules for coexistence between religious groups essential in that environment.[3]

As part of his effort to portray Eulogius as a cultured and educated person, Albar wrote enthusiastically about Eulogius's scholarship, praising his familiarity with both Christian and pagan Latin literature.[4] Eulogius journeyed to Pamplona in 850 and returned with a large number of books by Christian and pagan authors, including Augustine, Virgil, Juvenal, and Horace.[5] One of his scholarly activities while in prison was to reconstruct the quantity-based metrical rules governing classical Latin poetry.[6] The *Vita Eulogii* depicts Eulogius as a preserver of Latin culture, "correcting what had been corrupted, mending what was broken, restoring what was no longer used, reaffirming the value of the ancient."[7] Eulogius, Albar implies, was as *urbanus* as any Muslim but drew his learning from the Roman tradition rather than from the Islamic tradition which threatened to replace it.

The *Vita* also emphasizes that Eulogius was closely tied to the martyrs' movement long before his own arrest. Albar and Eulogius met while studying with Abbot Speraindeo, who had written a life of John and Adulphus, the two Christians who were executed in the 820s, so in a sense Eulogius was trained by an earlier chronicler of the movement.[8] Like many of the other martyrs, Eulogius was deeply involved in ascetic practices. He divided his time between priestly duties and extended retreats at local monasteries, where he practiced a strict ascetic regimen; he "burned with the fire of martyrdom."[9] Albar presents Eulogius's wish for martyrdom as a natural extension of his asceticism.

A few more biographical details about Eulogius emerge from his letter to Bishop Wiliesindus of Pamplona, whom Eulogius met on his journey north.[10] Eulogius wrote the letter while in prison in 851, to thank Wiliesindus for his hospitality and also to complain about the situation in Córdoba. The letter makes it clear that Eulogius's journey to Christian Pamplona influenced his thinking about the problems of Christians under Muslim rule. Eulogius spends much of the letter contrasting life in Christian Spain with life under an Islamic government. Christians in the north, he writes, are free to practice their religion as they like, while he is imprisoned because the authorities falsely believe that he incited the martyrdoms. In the north there are huge monasteries in which hundreds of monks sing psalms together; in Córdoba the only place one hears such singing is in jail.

The letter also provides some information about Eulogius's family. He writes that the original purpose of his journey was to search for two of his brothers who were, for unspecified reasons, living in exile in Bavaria. Eulogius was not able to get over the Pyrenees, however, because of a series of insurrections against Charles the Bald. Throughout his journey he was consumed with worry for his family, which was financially destitute at the time. When he returned to Córdoba, he found that his younger brother, who apparently held a position at court, had fallen into disfavor with the amir and been dismissed from government service.

For a man who never met a Muslim he liked, Eulogius had a surprising number of connections at court: a younger brother in government service, two other brothers who may have been exiled because of trouble with the Muslim authorities, and a counselor to the amir who knew Eulogius well. Eulogius wrote knowledgeably about the policies of Muhammad I, whom he disliked, commenting for example that the amir lacked his father's ability to control outlying provinces of al-Andalus and that he made himself unpopular by cutting his soldiers' pay.[11] These connections suggest that Eulogius's family had at one time enjoyed better relations with the Islamic government but had fallen from grace sometime before 850. Eulogius's relations with the Christian hierarchy in al-Andalus deteriorated at around the same time so that his imprisonment as a leader of the martyrs' movement occurred with the approval of Archbishop Reccafred. His falling-out with both Christian and Muslim authorities and the accompanying financial problems add a personal and material dimension to Eulogius's condemnation of Islam and of Christians he saw as collaborators with the Muslims.

The sources reveal less about Albar than about Eulogius, and what little information there is about Albar's life comes from his own writings. He seems to have been a layman[12] but was nevertheless a student of theology and Scripture and was, like Eulogius, a student of Abbot Speraindeo. In a letter to a man named Eleazar, a convert from Christianity to Judaism, Albar makes the interesting comment that he, Albar, is "of the family of Israel" (*ex Srahelis stirpe*) and "a Jew by faith and by race" (*et fide et gente Hebreus sum*) and that he therefore has a better right to call himself a Jew than Eleazar has.[13] The point of the letter is that Christians are the true

Jews because they recognized the Messiah when they saw him so it is difficult to say whether Albar is claiming literal or only metaphorical Jewish ancestry.

Other letters of Albar's reveal that he fell seriously ill, probably in the mid-850s, and that this illness caused him great troubles. One problem arose from his having received the sacrament of penance while ill.[14] The type of penance practiced in Córdoba at that time was the old form of public penance for mortal sin; it was considered to be a one-time-only measure so that even if the recipient lapsed back into mortal sin it could not be repeated. The penitent was expected to live the rest of his life according to a strict ascetic regimen, unable to marry, transact business, or take holy orders. If the sin was very serious, the recipient was temporarily denied communion; he could then be restored to communion through a public ceremony presided over by a bishop. Many Christians received penance only on their deathbeds to avoid the possibility of a relapse into sin.

Albar apparently received the sacrament on what he thought was his deathbed but then unexpectedly recovered. In such circumstances, according to the ruling of an episcopal council in Barcelona in 540, the recovered patient must live as a penitent and be barred from communion until he had demonstrated the capacity to lead a virtuous life.[15] Albar wrote several letters to Bishop Saul of Córdoba, asking to be readmitted to communion.[16] Saul refused, and the two argued bitterly.

Sometime after his illness, Albar wrote to an important personage at court named Romanus asking him for help with a legal problem.[17] Years before, Albar had granted a monastery certain rights over a part of his family's land, after which he and his father had sold the land. Around the time of his illness Albar decided to buy it back, but because various problems surrounded the transaction he asked an unidentified official at court to make the purchase on his behalf. Once he had purchased the land on Albar's behalf, however, the official demanded that Albar sell it to him, saying that he was entitled to it because of favors he had done for Albar in the past. Albar did sell to the official, apparently at a loss. Because the official refused to comply with the terms of Albar's donation to the monastery, the monastery was now suing Albar for breach of contract. In his letter, Albar explains to Romanus that he is too impoverished and too weak physically from his recent illness to oppose the official; his status as a penitent may also have prevented him from conducting business. He begs Romanus to intercede for him with a certain Count Servandus at court.

Romanus and Count Servandus both reappear in a later Christian source as highly placed and corrupt Christian courtiers, rich, decadent, and deeply assimilated to Islamic culture, just the sort of creatures against whom Albar directed much of his polemic.[18] His letter indicates that he was nevertheless willing to call upon such undesirables in an emergency, and he gushes obsequiously throughout the letter, reminding Romanus of the long history of love and friendship between their two families.

By the 850s, Albar, like Eulogius, had come into conflict with officials at court and with members of the Christian hierarchy. Both men had seen better days financially, and both had reason to resent those in power, Christians and Muslims alike.

Sources for the Defense of the Martyrs

The execution of Christians for denouncing Islam did not begin with the martyrs of the mid-850s. The most obvious precedent was the execution of Adulphus and John, about whom Speraindeo wrote in the 820s.

Middle Eastern sources may also have influenced Albar and Eulogius. One of those martyred at Córdoba, George, was a monk at the monastery of Mar Sabas in Jerusalem, the monastery where St. John of Damascus had lived one hundred years earlier and where he composed his anti-Islamic polemic.[19] An early life of St. John may have been written by the 850s, and in any event George could have told stories to Eulogius and the other confessors about his monastery's most famous resident.[20] Eulogius had direct contact with George, whom he reports delivered to him a letter from the monastery of Mar Sabas, which may have contained information about John of Damascus.

John of Damascus was not martyred, but his career and his relationship with the Islamic government of Syria show some interesting parallels with the life of the Cordovan martyr Isaac.[21] John's was a Christian family that had been in government service under Byzantine rule, and John's grandfather Mansur ibn Sargun probably helped negotiate terms of surrender with the Muslim invaders. (The grandfather may have adopted this Arab name after the conquest, or it may indicate that the family was Arab Christian.) The family remained Christian but continued in government service under the Umayyad caliphs. Under Caliph al-Hisham (724–43),

John abruptly resigned his post, entered a monastery, and began writing anti-Islamic polemic.[22]

Also in 743, around the same time John entered Mar Sabas, Bishop Peter of Maiuma in Syria was sentenced to death for denouncing Muhammad as a false prophet and a forerunner of the Antichrist.[23] George most likely knew about this event, although there is no evidence that he told Eulogius about it.

Syria in the 740s and Córdoba in the 850s were undergoing similar processes of Islamization. In the seventh century, Arab rulers attempted to maintain a strict correspondence between Arab and Muslim identity. To convert to Islam, a non-Arab had to become the client, or *mawla*, of an Arab tribe, a position that implied second-class status. By the early decades of the eighth century, however, the distinction between Arab and non-Arab Muslims had begun to break down, and under Umar II (717–20) non-Arab Muslims were granted legal and fiscal status equal to that of Arabs. Syria, and especially its capital Damascus, may have seen an increase in conversions in the decades after Umar II's rule similar to the increase that took place in Córdoba after the time of Abd al-Rahman II.

Again, there is no direct evidence that Eulogius and Albar knew anything about John's career or Peter's execution. It seems highly likely, however, that George had something to say about John, if not about Peter, and it is also likely that Eulogius and Albar were familiar with John's anti-Islamic polemic. If Eulogius did hear about John, the parallels between John's career and Isaac's must have struck him, and John's story may have influenced his account of Isaac's dramatic conversion to monastic life.

The primary tradition with which Eulogius and Albar were working, however, was not from the Islamic Middle East but from the Roman period. Their purpose in writing about the Cordovan Christians who were executed was to establish that they were not just unfortunate victims of the Islamic legal system but martyrs in the heroic tradition of the early church. Eulogius shaped his biographical sketches of the martyrs to support this point of view. A surviving tenth-century Spanish collection of martyrs' lives, which was probably similar to the collection available to Eulogius, indicates that both the tone and the content of his writings were influenced by that earlier tradition.[24] Some aspects of the Cordovan martyrdoms fit with the Roman pattern better than others, however, a problem Eulogius recognized.[25]

Eulogius's accounts of the martyrdoms follow the pattern of the earlier stories in certain general ways. He begins with an account of the confessor's virtuous life and the circumstances surrounding his or her arrest, then moves to the deposition before the authorities at which the martyr vigorously defends his or her faith, the confessor's imprisonment, and finally the execution. At the hearings before the Muslim authorities, Eulogius's martyrs often echo the otherworldly tone of their earlier counterparts; the Roman martyr Tibertius, for example, says that he does not fear death because "this world seems to be, but is not, while the next world seems not to be, but is," a theme echoed by several of the Cordovan martyrs.[26] And, as in the Roman tradition, the outside, non-Christian world is depicted as filled with material seductions. In the Spanish collection's version of the passion of Agnes, for example, the Roman magistrate promises her wealth and help in making an advantageous marriage if she will sacrifice to the Roman gods; the Muslim authorities made the sisters Nunilo and Alodia a similar offer.[27]

Eulogius used other Roman sources besides the Spanish collection of passion stories, and his reliance on earlier writers is most apparent in his treatment of women martyrs. In his accounts of many of the martyrs, male and female, Eulogius emphasizes that their asceticism indicates their fitness for martyrdom as well as serving as a sort of training for martyrdom. He treats the virginity of some of the women as part of that preparatory ascetic practice. Eulogius's linking of virginity with fitness for martyrdom is especially clear when he addresses Flora and Maria in the *Documentum martyriale,* in which he draws on Jerome's writings about virginity. Eulogius quotes from Jerome that "pleasure stains a woman's body, not violence."[28] He uses nuptial imagery freely, promising Flora and Maria that marriage with Christ will be their reward for martyrdom, closely echoing Jerome's promises to his protégée Eustochium that such a marriage will be her reward for remaining a virgin.[29] And he repeats a frequent theme of Jerome's writings on virginity: that virtue in women is spiritually supercharged precisely because women are weak and sinful; more than men, they have to overcome their natures. As Eulogius says of Flora and Maria, "They have forgotten the weakness of their sex."[30]

Eulogius seems also to have been drawing on the late fourth-century *Peristephanon* by the Spanish poet Prudentius. In that work, Prudentius describes how the virgin Eulalia of Merida, barely twelve years old, longed to become a martyr but was restrained by her parents. One night she set out from her home in secret:

She, hating to let herself be saved by keeping quiet and hanging back like a coward, opens the door by night with none to see, makes her escape through the enclosing fence, and then pursues her way across the wilds. With torn feet she passes over rough waste overgrown with briars, but she is accompanied by a troop of angels, and for all the gruesome silence of the night she still has light to guide her. . . . Stepping quickly all through the night she covers many a mile ere the eastern quarter opens up the sky; and in the morning presents herself haughtily at the seat of power.[31]

Eulogius's account of the virgin martyr Pomposa follows this scene closely. She also wanted to be martyred but was held back by the older nuns at her monastery. She slipped away one night when the gate was accidentally left open: "Approaching [the gate] in silence, and secretly opening the door, she went through the night's darkness illuminated by a heavenly light, and passing over the entire rough road in empty wilderness before this twilight, at dawn she entered the city, and without delay had herself brought before the judge's scrutiny."[32]

Eulogius writes in the *Documentum martyriale* that Flora and Maria were given a choice between professing Islam and being sold into prostitution.[33] The theme of the prosecutor threatening to force a Christian virgin into prostitution is common in the literature of martyrdom. Prudentius's account of Agnes's death in the *Peristephanon* centers on such a threat, and Ambrose describes a similar case in his *De Virginibus,* to name just two works with which Eulogius was familiar.[34]

In some cases Eulogius may have adjusted the facts to fit his models, especially when he puts words into the mouths of the confessors or comments on their motives. The situation is complicated because the confessors who came out of the monasteries probably knew the same stories and were in fact modeling their behavior after earlier Christian examples.[35] Beyond such deliberate modeling, however, there were some genuine similarities between the martyrdoms of the Roman period and those taking place in Córdoba. The pattern of arrest, trial, and execution resembled that of Roman times. It is perfectly credible that a Christian from either period would speak of the next world when faced with imminent death. Christian attitudes toward virginity and women's spirituality had remained constant enough that Jerome's words still seemed relevant. And like Roman pagan society, Islamic society constituted a political authority and a materially seductive culture that were often in conflict with Christian values.

Eulogius made the most of such parallels wherever he found them, and he was certainly not above stretching the truth in deference to his models. He was, however, unwilling to do too much violence to the facts or else felt that he could not get away with a completely fictionalized version of the executions in Córdoba; he was writing at least partly for a contemporary audience, for Christians who disagreed with his views but knew the basic events surrounding the executions. Considerations of audience meant that Eulogius had to confront aspects of the martyrdoms which did not fit with his models at all. Eulogius then had to choose between reinterpreting the events—showing that they really did fit the model if they were studied in the proper light—or reinterpreting the model.

In his defense of the martyrs, Eulogius outlines the arguments of Christians who denied the legitimacy of the martyrdoms: Those executed died quickly and did not suffer torture as the Roman martyrs did. Martyrs of the Roman period were associated with miracles, which won many converts to Christianity, while the alleged martyrs of Córdoba could produce no miracles. The Roman government actively sought out and persecuted Christians, while Cordovan Christians generally were executed only after drawing attention to themselves. Romans were pagans and tried to force the confessors to sacrifice to idols, while in Córdoba the apostate confessors were asked to practice a monotheistic religion not unlike Christianity; in Eulogius's words, "People say that [the martyrs] suffered at the hands of men who worship God and the law, nor did they die invited to participate in the sacrileges of idols, but in a cult of the true God."[36]

Eulogius briskly dismisses the question of suffering. Suffering, Eulogius argues, is a subjective phenomenon, and nothing is worse than death. What could be more terrible than to look upon the sword that is about to lop off your head?[37]

The question of miracles cannot be so easily dispatched. Eulogius and Albar both claimed that some miracles did in fact occur—a thunderstorm after one execution and the death by drowning of a group of Muslims who had just witnessed Perfectus's execution.[38]Albar reports that after Eulogius and Leocritja were executed and their bodies thrown into the river, a dove landed on Eulogius's body and refused to move, and Leocritja's corpse would not sink.[39] This last image, of Eulogius's and Leocritja's headless bodies floating in the river, seems sad rather than trium-

phant, and none of the "miracles" Eulogius reports could be expected
to bring about mass conversions. Eulogius recognized the problem and
tried to reinterpret the Roman model by arguing that miracles are not all
that important; one should admire the virtue of those who perform the
miracles, not the miracles themselves.[40] He conveys the idea that miracles
are flashy and tasteless and that Córdoba's martyrs were all the holier for
eschewing them.[41]

Christians opposed to the martyrs' movement argued that the Muslims
did nothing to provoke the martyrdoms; instead, the martyrs provoked
the Muslim authorities and brought down a wave of persecution on the
Christian community. Eulogius and Albar responded to that objection by
arguing that a persecution of sorts was going on even before the martyrdoms began. Priests were harassed in the street; restrictions prohibiting
Christians from openly preaching the gospel or expressing opinions about
Islam were sources of humiliation. As Albar puts it, "What could be a
greater persecution, what more severe kind of degradation is to be feared
than when a person cannot say in public what he believes by reason in his
heart?"[42] One of their tactics, then, was to redefine persecution as a situation that forced Christians to present an outer, public person whose behavior conflicted with the inner, private person, a definition that particularly fit the experience of those martyrs who were secret Christians. Albar
also vehemently rejected the idea that the martyrs themselves worsened
the situation of Christians in Córdoba by their extreme actions. He argued
that it was the Muslims who intensified the persecutions when they broke
faith with Perfectus, and he suggested that their later retaliatory measures
should be seen not as a result of the martyrs' intemperance but as a punishment from God against Christians who did not support the martyrs.[43]

Eulogius and Albar also argued that Islam was so vile, so immoral, and
so false in all its beliefs that its very existence called the good Christian to
protest, whether or not Muslims were carrying out an active persecution.
This argument also answered another objection that Christians raised
against the legitimacy of the martyrs: that Muslims were not pagans and
that living among Muslims was not so terrible. Islam, Eulogius and Albar
contended, was a danger because it tempted Christians to an immoral way
of life. If Christians tolerated the existence of such a competing form of
religion, it would automatically reduce the strength of Christianity.[44]

Given the cosmopolitan environment of Córdoba, that was a radical
argument. Albar and Eulogius did not simply urge Christians to resist

obvious forms of persecution; they suggested that the very existence of
Islam constituted a kind of persecution and should be unacceptable to
any right-thinking Christian. In making such a radical argument the two
authors moved into a defense of the martyrs that went well beyond drawing parallels with Roman models.

Against Islam

Eulogius and Albar wrote in part for Christians who believed that Islam
was a legitimate religion that worshiped the true God and who felt that
it was perfectly acceptable for Christians to live alongside Muslims. Their
argument against this tolerant point of view works at different levels,
from scriptural analysis to personal attacks against Muslims in general and
Muhammad in particular.

At the heart of Eulogius's and Albar's polemic is a simple but powerful idea: the one fact about Islam that should make it unacceptable to any
right-thinking Christian is that Islam is not Christianity. Muslims do not
believe in the divinity of Christ. Because Muslims are not Christians, no
aspect of their beliefs can be divinely inspired. Christianity is the only
true religion. The Gospel was preached all over the world so all peoples
had their chance; anyone who did not accept the truth of the Gospel is
damned.[45] This argument is not as simple-minded as it might seem. In
a city in which religious pluralism had been tolerated for more than a
century, Albar's and Eulogius's insistence upon the universality of Christianity and its sole claim to religious legitimacy was innovative.

Again, one should bear in mind that Albar and Eulogius addressed a
group of Christians who did not see much difference between Christianity and Islam. The authors' arguments indicate that there was at least
some consensus among Christians and Muslims in Córdoba on doctrinal
matters—even on the issue of Christ's nature, which one would expect
to be a source of division between the two groups.

Jesus is an important figure in Islam, second only to Muhammad in his
authority as a prophet.[46] He is not considered to be divine, but the Quran
does confirm that he was born to a virgin.[47] In addition, by the ninth
century a *hadith* was generally accepted which states that all babies are
squeezed at birth by Satan (that is why they cry), but that Mary and Jesus
escaped this contact with the devil; behind this tradition seems to lie an
echo of the immaculate conception. At several points the Quran refers
to Jesus as the "word of God."[48] Standard Muslim interpretations make it

clear that this "word" is not to be interpreted as the *logos;* Jesus was the word of God in the sense that he was conceived not by intercourse but by God's word or in the sense that he himself preached God's word.

Although the Quran and later Muslim interpreters are careful to reject the idea of Christ's divinity, there are similarities between Christian and Muslim views of Jesus: his importance as a prophet, his freedom from sin, the unique nature of his conception, his status as the word of God (whatever one takes that to mean). Albar and Eulogius were aware of these similarities. Eulogius recognized that Muslims acknowledge Jesus as the word of God (*verbum dei*).[49] Albar reports that Christians who did not wish to draw attention to their religious identity talked about Jesus as the *verbum dei*.[50] This formulation of Jesus' status emphasized the continuities rather than the differences between Christian and Muslim beliefs, and it also had the advantage of being vague; Muslims and Christians could both use the phrase "word of God" while meaning rather different things by it.

Some sources suggest that Christians in Córdoba had gone beyond a certain vagueness concerning theological issues and had actually adjusted their concept of Christ to accommodate Islamic beliefs. Eulogius and Albar's teacher Speraindeo wrote a letter, at Albar's request, refuting a heresy current at the time of the martyrs' movement.[51] The heretics in question, according to Albar, did not believe in Christ's divinity; if he was divine, they ask, then why did he say in John 20.17, "I am now ascending to my father and your father, to my God and your God"? In his letter Speraindeo addresses the problem of Christ's divinity at some length and also refutes misconceptions about the trinity which Albar alleged were part of the group's beliefs.[52] Regarding the specific passage from John cited by the heretics, Speraindeo argues that Christ has two natures within a single person and that he was speaking of his human nature when he announced that he was ascending to his father.

Letters 1 through 6 of the Albar correspondence, between John of Seville and Albar, suggest that there may have been Adoptionists among the Cordovan Christians.[53] The chief proponent of Adoptionism in al-Andalus was Elipandus, who became archbishop of Toledo around 783. Adoptionists believed in a strong division between Christ's divine and human natures and in his double sonship; insofar as he is divine, he is God's natural son, but insofar as he is human, he is God's adopted son. This belief spread into Carolingian territory along the Spanish March, where it came to the attention of Charlemagne's court and was vigorously attacked by Alcuin. In 794 the Council of Frankfurt formally condemned Adoptionism, decreeing that there is only one son and that he is not adopted.

Adoptionism was very close to Nestorianism in its understanding of Christ and may have been transmitted by Nestorian Syrians who came with the Umayyads to al-Andalus. It also represented a compromise between orthodox Christian and Islamic views of Christ.[54] Nestorians distinguished strongly between Christ's two natures because they were interested in his humanity, his life on earth; they emphasized that he was the perfect man and a model for others.[55] This emphasis may have been attractive to Christians in al-Andalus because it came close to a Muslim view of Christ, and it also makes Christ sound very much like Muhammad, who according to Muslim teachings was a perfect model of human virtue. At the same time, though, Adoptionists (like Nestorians) recognized that Christ also had a divine nature, and thus they avoided jettisoning an essential Christian belief.

The extent to which Cordovan Christians had embraced Adoptionism or the even more unorthodox views discussed by Albar and Speraindeo is impossible to gauge. It is clear, though, that some Christians in Córdoba saw more similarities than differences between Islam and Christianity and that Muslims and Christians had developed ways of talking about their beliefs without offending each other. For Eulogius and Albar, any blurring of the differences between the two religions was a betrayal of Christianity; they saw it as their mission to eradicate such fuzzy-mindedness and put an end to the possibility of civil discourse between Christians and Muslims.

The crudest, and in some ways the most powerful, aspect of their efforts to discredit Islam and distinguish it from Christianity consists of attacks on what Eulogius and Albar perceived to be the immorality of Muhammad and his teachings. They argue that Muhammad was a deeply corrupt man who taught his followers to imitate his immorality; he therefore cannot have founded a true religion.

Eulogius quotes from a life of Muhammad, which he says he found in Pamplona.[56] Muhammad was an orphan, a moneylender by profession, and married to a widow. He committed to memory bits of teachings he had heard from Christians. A demon appeared to him in the form of a vulture with a golden mouth; he mistook the demon for the angel Gabriel and, on the instructions of the demon began preaching, urging people to stop worshiping idols and instead to worship a corporeal god in heaven.

He ordered his followers to kill all nonbelievers. He seduced Zaynab, the
wife of his follower Zayd, then pretended to receive a scriptural passage
from God condoning this behavior. When Muhammad was near death he
told his followers that Gabriel would raise him up on the third day. Instead his body rotted and was eaten by dogs.

Like all of Eulogius's and Albar's information about Muhammad, this
biography is a bizarre combination of what to a Muslim would have
passed for distorted fact—Muhammad was married to a widow named
Khadija, he did claim to have received his initial revelation from Gabriel,
and there are verses in the Quran which address Zaynab's divorce from
Zayd and subsequent marriage to Muhammad—mixed with grotesque
invention: the vulture-demon, the dogs, and in particular Muhammad's
claim that he would return from the dead.

Albar writes about Muhammad's alleged sexual promiscuity.[57] He repeats the story about Muhammad's seduction of Zaynab; he refers to
Muhammad as a womanizer (*femellarius*) and says Muslims boast that
Muhammad had the potency of forty men. Because of Muhammad's example, all Muslim men are adulterers, having three or four wives or concubines. Albar also claims that Muslims go against natural law with their
wives but adds that modesty commands him to remain silent on this
point, thus allowing his reader to imagine something truly colorful. Even
Muhammad's paradise is sexual, populated by whores who will miraculously be restored to virginity after each act of intercourse.

Muhammad, according to Albar, was so successful because he made
religion sound easy and used only pleasing words. He did not teach a
doctrine of the spirit, but rather a doctrine addressing only concerns of
the body, such as bathing. While Christ taught peace, Muhammad taught
men to fight; Christ taught virginity and chastity, Muhammad incest and
pleasure; Christ taught fasting, Muhammad gluttony.[58]

Such personal attacks against Muhammad, and particularly charges of
sexual misconduct, have precursors among Middle Eastern writers. Franz
Franke notes that similar characterizations of Muhammad and of Muslims appear in a ninth-century work by the Christian apologist al-Kindi
and suggests that he and the Cordovan authors were drawing on a common source of Middle Eastern origin.[59] The Cordovan polemic also shares
elements with John of Damascus's description of Islam; John wrote that
the "superstition of Islam" was a "fore-runner of the Antichrist," and he
recorded the story about Muhammad's seduction of Zaynab.[60]

Eulogius and Albar combined attacks against Muhammad and Muslims in general with similar criticisms of Muslims who were their contemporaries in Córdoba. These criticisms were an integral part of their condemnation of Islam: a set of beliefs that produced such an undesirable group of people could not possibly be a true religion. The attacks on contemporaries are remarkably bitter and express the authors' feelings that they were abused and culturally overshadowed by the Muslim presence in Córdoba.

Both authors express their sense of Islam overwhelming them and literally drowning them out in their description of the muezzin's call to prayer. They write that the muezzin's yelling enraged and demoralized Christians (or at least good Christians). Eulogius reports that some Christians put their fingers in their ears when they heard the call to prayer; his grandfather, also named Eulogius, always fortified himself with the sign of the cross and sang psalms to cover the sound of the muezzin's voice.[61] Albar describes the muezzin in deeply hostile terms: "They scream this [the call to prayer] out daily in smoky towers with a monstrous elephant's trumpeting, with the wide-open mouth of beasts, and the loose lips and wide-open gullet of people with belly aches."[62]

Muslims are deceptive and seductive in their speech and writing. Albar argues that Christians like to read books in Arabic only because they are written with fluency and eloquence; the sound of what they say in Arabic is pleasing but lacks real meaning. He quotes from Gregory the Great that "in the manner of metal chimes they have the meaningless sound of speaking well, but have no understanding of living well."[63]

Muslims are proud and mean and are especially abusive to priests. When they see a priest in the street, they shout insults, throw rocks, and sing bawdy songs (cantica inhonesta).[64] Eulogius writes that "many of them consider it a defilement if we [priests] touch so much as their clothing."[65] If, as the sources suggest, many Christians had adopted Muslim dress, then a priest in robes would furnish an obvious target for harassment.

Albar summarizes the obnoxious characteristics of Muslims:

Muslims are puffed up with pride, languid in their enjoyment of fleshly acts, extravagant in eating, greedy usurpers in the acquisition of possessions and the pillaging of the poor, grasping without piety, liars without shame, deceitful without discernment, wanton without modesty, cruel without mercy, usurpers without justice, without honor, without truth, unfamiliar with kindness or compassion, ignorant of the humility of piety, fickle, fashion-conscious [*ornati*], crafty, cunning, and indeed not halfway but completely befouled in the dregs of every impiety, deriding humility as insanity, rejecting chastity as though it were filth, disparaging virginity as though it were the uncleanness of harlotry, putting the vices of the body before the virtues of the soul, advertising their characteristic way of life through their acts and deportment.[66]

The modern reader can easily dismiss this polemic as hateful and willfully ignorant of Islam and Arab culture. The attacks on Islam are often petty and personal; Albar's characterization of Muslims as "usurpers" (*invasores*) seems aimed specifically at the court official who stole his land. The general tone of the polemic, particularly Albar's, borders on the hysterical. It would be wrong, however, to underestimate the calculation and intelligence behind the authors' seemingly wild rhetoric.

Eulogius's and Albar's ignorance of Islam was discretionary; their knowledge varied from moment to moment, depending on the specific argument they wished to support. Eulogius, as we have seen, gives a fairly nuanced explanation of Muslim beliefs about Jesus. He also makes some statements that are clearly inaccurate, such as his contention that Muhammad commanded Muslims to kill all unbelievers, a statement Eulogius's own presence in Córdoba proves false. Eulogius and Albar were not ethnologists or historians. Islam, in their view, had no right to exist, and any argument that could convince Christians of that fact was valid, whether or not it was accurate.

Most of the Cordovan anti-Islamic polemic consists of neither accurate statements about Islam nor pure fabrications but is a clever twisting of Muslim beliefs. Islam does allow divorce and polygamy. Both the Quran and popular stories depict paradise as a place of sensual as well as spiritual pleasures, but in the Islamic tradition those images do not carry the implication of sin or excess as they do in Christianity. Muslim law, or *sharia,* does place an emphasis on outward expressions of piety, like the ritual performance of ablutions; so that Albar is not completely wrong in claiming that Islam cares about the things of the body, such as bathing (clearly a reference to ablutions). Within Islam, sufis often voiced the same complaint about *sharia.* But such outward practices are meant to cultivate an inward sense of prayerfulness; they are not ends in themselves. Eulogius and Albar represented the forms of Islamic practice fairly accurately (at least some of the time) but deliberately misrepresented its content.

The Cordovan authors' limited view of Islam reflects the fact that they were interested in only one narrow aspect of Islamic culture: court culture. The forms of misconduct they ascribed to Muslims and assimilated Christians were caused by the excesses associated with life at the top: too much food, sex, wine, and money. Eulogius and Albar accused Muslims of offenses associated with power: cruelty, rudeness, arrogance, and a general contempt for those over whom they held authority. The authors may have been aware that there were other dimensions to Islam, but their polemic attacked only Muslims who held political power.

Finally, it would be wrong to dismiss out of hand Eulogius's and Albar's claim that Christians in Córdoba were persecuted. The situation was not, as the authors claimed, comparable to the Roman persecution of Christians. Nevertheless, *dhimmi*s were not legally or socially equal to Muslims. They were always vulnerable—to a ruler who suddenly decided to enforce the rules of the *dhimma* to the letter or to casual ridicule and abuse. When Eulogius describes how Muslim children taunted priests with obscene songs and threw rocks at them, he seems to speak from his own experience. *Dhimmi* status also made one more vulnerable to other abuses the authors and their families had experienced—sudden dismissal from a job at court or being cheated by an official. Eulogius's and Albar's depiction of Muslims in power is surely exaggerated, but it may be true that the court attracted men who were ambitious and ruthless, particularly in their treatment of the powerless.

In creating a stereotype of Islam, Eulogius and Albar also created an ideal image of Christianity. If Muslims were proud, luxury-loving, sexually depraved, and violent, then Christians must be humble, ascetic, celibate, and peace-loving. One strong contrast this polemic sought to draw was between the worldliness of Islam and the profound otherworldliness of Christianity. This is a simplistic distinction, but there is some truth to it: Islam is in some respects more reconciled to this world than Christianity is, or at least than medieval Catholicism was.[67] This kernel of truth must have seemed particularly compelling in Córdoba, where a Muslim elite ruled over a Christian subject population; the powerful have good reason to appreciate the world as it is.

In his *Kitab al-qudat bi Qurtuba*, al-Khushani takes an ironic view of radical Christian claims to spiritual superiority. He records the story of a Christian who came before the *qadi* in around 920, "seeking his own death."[68] The story's narrator explains that Christians believed this sort of suicide to be a pious act, although Jesus had never encouraged any such thing. The *qadi* reprimanded the Christian for trying to commit suicide; the Christian replied that it would not be he who was killed but only "my image" (*shabhi*), "while I myself will go to heaven." The *qadi* had him whipped, then asked him on whose back the whip had fallen. "On mine," the Christian replied. "Just as the sword will fall on your neck," said the *qadi*. This story suggests that Cordovan Muslims thought of radical Christians as almost Manichaean in their insistence upon a separation between body and spirit.

Eulogius and Albar aimed their polemic primarily at fellow Cordovan Christians who had failed to appreciate the seriousness of their situation. At times, though, they seem to have a wider audience in mind— Christians outside of Córdoba, even outside of al-Andalus, or perhaps posterity in general. Eulogius was more skillful at writing for a general audience than Albar. Whereas Albar's writing is often confusing and his point lost in invective, Eulogius explains events relatively clearly and tries to provide the background information that someone from outside of al-Andalus would need. One small example of his awareness of an outside audience occurs when he describes the arrest of two martyrs who preached the Gospel in a mosque; the Muslims, Eulogius writes, consider it a grave offense for Christians to create a disturbance in a mosque.[69] No Christian living under Islamic rule would need such an explanation.

Eulogius wanted outsiders to know about conditions in Córdoba. The earliest evidence we have of his outreach program is his letter of 851 to Wiliesindus, in which he describes the martyrs' movement up to that point; he also no doubt discussed the problems of Cordovan Christians during his trip north. Albar reports one very dramatic result of this communication with the outside: Eulogius was elected bishop of Toledo, by a council of bishops, but was unable to occupy the see because of "obstacles placed in his way."[70] Presumably the election occurred after Eulogius had visited Toledo, although Albar gives no date. Because Albar writes so briefly of this event and no other source mentions it, it is difficult to know what to make of it. It seems very strange that a Cordovan priest who had visited Toledo only briefly should be elected bishop. One possible explanation is that once Eulogius began traveling and meeting people, he seized the opportunity to propagandize about the horrors of conditions in Córdoba; his trip north may have been his first opportunity to package and present his feelings about Christian life in Córdoba. Perhaps he was perceived as a heroic victim of Muslim persecution. Another possibility is that since Christian and Muslim magnates around Toledo were often in rebellion against the Cordovan government, the election of someone so obviously critical of the Cordovan regime appealed to them as a good opportunity to flout the amir's authority.

Word of the martyrdoms had certainly spread outside of Córdoba by 858. In that year two monks from Paris arrived in Córdoba and took home the relics of three of the martyrs. An account of their journey was written by a colleague upon their return to the monastery.[71]

The monks did not originally intend to come to Córdoba. They initially crossed the Pyrenees because they had heard that St. Vincent's relics were available in Valencia; it turned out that these had already been moved to Saragossa, however, where they were being venerated as the relics of a completely different saint. While the monks were in Barcelona, a court official and the bishop of Barcelona told them about the executions in Córdoba. Not wishing to return home with no relics, they headed south. In Córdoba they met Eulogius himself and heard more about the martyrs. Much of their time in Córdoba was taken up with negotiations for the relics of George and Aurelius, who were buried under the altar at the monastery of Pinna Mellaria. (In the process of negotiation, the monks learned that the monastery had Aurelius's body and his wife Sabigotho's head, a mix-up that occurred because their bodies had to be collected at night by stealth. The author explains this at some length, perhaps to forestall any criticism of his colleagues or the relics they had collected.) The monks of the monastery were, not surprisingly, unwilling to give up the martyrs' remains—the Muslims tried to prevent Christians from obtaining the bodies of the martyrs so that relics were in short supply—and the French monks obtained them only after Bishop Saul ordered the monastery to hand them over. After a lengthy and difficult journey, the monks arrived back in France, where they related stories about the martyrs to Charles the Bald.[72]

The monks' visit to Córdoba provided an excellent opportunity for Eulogius to spread word of the martyrs beyond the Iberian Peninsula. As far as can be determined from the travel narrative, the French monks came into contact exclusively with antiassimilationist Christians who supported the martyrs: Abbot Samson of Pinna Mellaria, who wrote a treatise excoriating Christians at the Muslim court; Leovigildus, who was probably the author of *De habitu clericorum,* a treatise urging clergy to dress in full robes even though doing so might incur Muslim hostility; and of course Eulogius. The monks left Córdoba with Eulogius's version of events; it is Eulogius's perceptions of the martyrs' movement which are reflected in the travel account and which the monks no doubt communicated in France.

The extent to which the French monks had absorbed Eulogius's point of view is evidenced by the large number of miracles the martyrs' relics performed on the journey back to France.[73] Eulogius was unable to impose his interpretation of the executions on all of the Cordovan Christian community; the events he describes were too recent, complex, and controversial.[74] As a result, the martyrs' relics could not perform a single credible miracle in Córdoba. Yet once removed from that skeptical environment, they began to heal the sick and strike down miscreants at a rapid pace. Outside of Córdoba, the martyrs became what Eulogius wished them to be: heroes of the church killed by savage oppressors. Within Córdoba, the complex social and cultural issues behind Eulogius's polemic were too evident for most people to accept it at face value.

4

Christians as the Enemy

Albar's and Eulogius's polemic was directed against Christians as well as against Muslims, specifically against those who in the authors' view were bad Christians. Bad Christians, according to Eulogius and Albar, were those who worked with Muslims, adopted Muslim practices, and opposed the actions of the martyrs. Good Christians supported the martyrs, maintained distinctively Christian practices, and had nothing to do with Muslims. All of the polemic was aimed at Christians because the authors could not reasonably have expected that Muslims would read their works. Their attacks on Islam were not intended to persuade Muslims to convert but to persuade Christians to stop associating with Muslims.

The Cordovan authors attacked in a general way Christians who thoughtlessly adopted certain aspects of Muslim culture in order to get along in the world, regarding the differences between Islam and Christianity as trivial. They aimed more specific criticisms against Christians who worked for the Islamic government. Such Christians adopted the style of life of their Muslim colleagues and sometimes converted to Islam. That deeply compromised group of Christians included members of the church hierarchy, who, from the perspective of radical Christians, were guilty of collaborating with the Islamic authorities and failing to support the martyrs.

Albar was particularly infuriated by Christians who passed for Muslim.

This passing took various forms. The secret Christians whom Eulogius describes professed one religion in public and another in private. Others simply did not draw attention to the fact that they were Christian; the merchant John was accused by Muslims in the marketplace of allowing his customers to assume that he was Muslim but not of actually claiming to be Muslim.[1]

To most Christians, such a minor subterfuge was probably just common sense; because laws requiring distinctive dress of non-Muslims were rarely enforced, there was no reason to draw attention to one's second-class status as a *dhimmi*. To Eulogius and Albar, however, passing was a serious matter, perhaps even a form of apostasy. Both were deeply opposed to the idea that it is possible to be one thing outwardly and another inwardly. People who passed were fooling only themselves if they believed they were real Christians: "In public before the pagans they do not pray, they do not fortify themselves with the sign of the cross when they yawn; they declare Christ to be God not openly before them but only in disguised utterances, in which they assert that Christ is the word and spirit of God, as [the Muslims] claim, preserving their own beliefs in their heart, as for a God who sees all."[2] This criticism was aimed at Christians who saw no substantive difference between Christians and Muslims, even in the two groups' understanding of Jesus. The passage also illuminates the radical Christian authors' definition of persecution: persecution exists when one cannot outwardly affirm one's inner beliefs.

Stronger condemnation was reserved for Christians who had become courtiers. One of the dangers Islam posed, according to Eulogius and Albar, was that it could corrupt Christians and make them just as bad as Muslims, and this was a particular danger for Christians at court. Eulogius describes the highly placed Christian official who denounced him at the episcopal council in the same words Albar uses to criticize Muslims; the official is "unjust, arrogant, proud, domineering, and unscrupulous."[3] Albar offers a series of complaints about Christians at court: they undergo circumcision to avoid Muslim scorn and learn to speak and read Arabic instead of Latin; they ingratiate themselves with Muslims so they can earn large salaries, amass money and jewels, eat well, and wear fine clothes.[4]

A slightly later work, the *Apologeticus,* written in 864 by Abbot Samson of the monastery of Pinna Mellaria, gives a similar view of Christians at court.[5] Samson, like Eulogius and Albar, had close ties to the martyrs' movement. He had at one time been associated with the Basilica of St.

Zoilus, where Eulogius was a priest. In 858 he became abbot of Pinna Mellaria, which housed the relics of Aurelius, George, and Sabigotho. Its possession of relics probably made Pinna Mellaria an important place in the eyes of the martyrs' supporters because the government tried to prevent Christians from obtaining the bodies of those who were executed.

Also like Eulogius and Albar, Samson's connections at court had deteriorated by the time he began writing about the situation in Córdoba.[6] He had at one time been in favor at the court and in the early 860s had been entrusted with the job of translating sensitive letters intended for the Frankish king from Arabic to Latin. Around that time, however, Samson's position at court came under attack. He was accused of trying to pass the amir's military secrets to the Franks in his translations. He was also accused of urging other Christians to denounce Muhammad, an action that would have been tantamount to inciting a new martyrs' movement. Not only Muslims at court but fellow Christians turned on Samson. Bishop Hostegesis of Malaga accused Samson of heresy before a council of bishops in 862. Two years later the amir called another church council, at which the charges were renewed. (Samson notes that Jews and Muslims appointed by the amir attended the council.) The council also deposed Samson's close friend Valentius, who had been bishop of Córdoba, and replaced him with a man named Stefanus, whom Samson regarded as a puppet of the amir. At that point, having concluded that his position in Córdoba was untenable, Samson took refuge in Martos and wrote the *Apologeticus*, in which he attacks his enemies and defends the orthodoxy of his own views.

Much of the *Apologeticus* is concerned with the highly technical theological dispute between Samson and his enemies, but the section of most historical interest is the preface to book 2, in which Samson launches an exceptionally spirited personal attack against prominent courtiers. Hostegesis is his primary target. Hostegesis, according to Samson, is a simoniac and an enemy to all Christians. Bishops were normally entitled to take one-third of all pious donations in their diocese for repairs to churches and relief of the poor, but Hostegesis extorted far more and spent the money on presents for the amir's sons and other courtiers, with whom he drank himself sick. He and his cronies engaged in boasting matches to determine who was the most depraved. He took a census of Christians in his diocese, then turned the names over to the palace to be used as tax rolls. One day he failed to celebrate the vesper office of the Virgin because he was waiting on one of the amir's most important courtiers, Hashim ibn Abd al-Aziz. The gates to his home were always guarded while Christians went hungry outside. Clerics under his control who refused to pay taxes were dragged naked through the streets.

Hostegesis's elderly father, Avurnus, was also at court; just as many of the good Christians, the martyrs, were related to each other, the bad Christians were also linked by blood. Avurnus had apostasized to Islam, in part to avoid prosecution for stealing from the Christian community. As part of his conversion, Avurnus became circumcised, which arouses Samson's most particular disgust; he imagines the operation in graphic detail, describing how Avurnus allowed his graying pubic hair and aging genitalia to be placed in the hands of the surgeon and speculating on the problems the surgeon had in cutting through Avurnus's tough old foreskin.

Eulogius and Albar also condemned the practice of circumcision for Christians. Albar argues that a Christian who becomes circumcised has despised the circumcision of the heart in favor of circumcision of the body.[7] He has, in other words, done exactly the opposite of what St. Paul recommended: he has ignored the inner man in favor of outward ritual. Once again, Albar argues that Islam is a collection of outward practices with no inner content.

To Samson and Albar, circumcision represented everything that was reprehensible about Christians at court. It was a physical mark of collaboration with the enemy; Albar says that circumcised Christians have taken on the mark of the Antichrist.[8] A later Christian source reports that Muslims insisted that their Christian colleagues be circumcised,[9] and the willingness of Avurnus and others to undergo the operation as adults suggests that it was crucial to their acceptance at court. Foreskin, or its absence, was a clear sign of where one's loyalties lay.

An uncle of Hostegesis's was also at court. He had been bishop of Granada but was deposed; he then obtained a position at court, which he used to persecute fellow Christians and put priests in jail. Samson refers to him as the new Judas Iscariot and notes that he was already circumcised before he came to Córdoba and thus fell in easily with the Muslims at court.

The courtier Servandus was related to Hostegesis by marriage. Samson particularly disliked Servandus and in describing him uses almost the same words Eulogius and Albar use to condemn Muslims and corrupt Christians: greedy, arrogant, rapacious, and cruel. In an apparent effort to encourage criminal prosecution of the martyrs' supporters, Servandus removed relics of the martyrs from beneath church altars and brought the mutilated bodies before the amir's men, demanding punishment for those who had preserved the bodies contrary to the amir's orders. His harshness against Christians was so great that many apostasized to Islam.

Samson tells us that Servandus was from a family of former slaves. His connections at court, then, make him an upstart; he could not claim to be from an "old senatorial family," as Eulogius could. Hostegesis, according to Samson, was also an uncultured person; Samson devotes a long section of the *Apologeticus* to an analysis of the written charges of heresy Hostegesis had brought against him and takes particular pleasure in enumerating Hostegesis's errors in spelling and case endings: "So come along, I pray, all of you who know Latin, and if you are strong enough, restrain your laughter, which I cannot." [10]

Two of Servandus's cronies at court were Romanus (very possibly the same one to whom Albar wrote for help with a lawsuit) and Sebastianus, who were father and son. Samson accuses these two of carrying on sexual liaisons with the palace eunuchs and with a variety of concubines.

Later in book 2 Samson outlines the theological dispute between Hostegesis and himself, seeking to demonstrate that Hostegesis and his friends were the real heretics. [11] Hostegesis had condemned Samson for holding that God is everywhere, in all material and spiritual being. Hostegesis contended that it was blasphemous to say that God is present in vermin, for example, or where sin is taking place; God remains in heaven and is in creation not *per substantiam* but *per subtilitatem*. In reply, Samson argues, echoing St. Augustine, that all being is good because God created it and that God is therefore present in all of it. To suggest that God is "located" in heaven is a kind of anthropomorphism, suggesting that God has a physical body.

Like most participants in the conflicts of ninth-century Córdoba, Samson and his opponents understood their dispute largely in religious terms; upward of 95 percent of the *Apologeticus* argues the question of who is a heretic and who is a real Christian, showing that this level of the dispute was of utmost importance to Samson and his contemporaries. Other issues were at stake, however. One was power. Samson argues that evil and incompetent men have gained control over fellow Christians and over the administration of the church. These men are heretics. They exploit the Christian community. They do not have the family background or erudition that would make them deserving of their power; they are vulgar, of low birth, and cannot tell a dative case ending from a nominative. Samson faults Hostegesis's writing for *rusticitas,* among many other things, and worries that ignorance such as his will destroy all knowledge of Latin grammar in Spain.[12]

The Muslim conquest in Spain, as in other areas, shattered existing power relationships. Connections within the Islamic government now helped determine one's access to power. The disputes among ninth-century Cordovan Christians were fueled by a complex mixture of theological and practical issues, but they were at one level disputes between men like Hostegesis who had profited from their contact with the court and men like Samson, Eulogius, and Albar who had not. The concern the last three showed for Latin letters came out of a desire to preserve the Latin Christian tradition against the encroachment of Islamic culture, but their focus on Latin high culture was also a means of showing that it was they, with their education and their cultivated writing style, who should be in charge.

The *Apologeticus* also highlights the extent to which Christians who opposed assimilation saw Islam not as a legitimate competing religious system but as a lack of religion, a surrender to sensuality. For Samson, as for Albar and Eulogius, sexual conduct was an extremely important dividing line between good Christians on the one hand and Muslims and Christians who had been influenced by Islam on the other. True Christians were ascetics; Muslims and Christians at court indulged in every manner of sexual license. Samson presents a sharp contrast between courtiers like Romanus and Sebastianus, with their omnivorous sexual proclivities, and Samson's friend Bishop Valentius, whom he describes as "adorned with virginity and dedicated to abstinence."

It is possible that the charges of treason against Samson were true, although he hotly denies them, and in any case Christians working in government were natural targets for accusations of that sort. It is also possible that Samson's sympathy for the martyrs made him an object of suspicion. Samson was never a full-time courtier—he was abbot of Pinna Mellaria at the time he was asked to translate the amir's letters—but he held a position of trust at that point. That trust quickly evaporated, for whatever reason, and Samson was forced to flee Córdoba. The similarities to Eulogius's and Albar's experiences of the world of the court are obvious. Once he had run afoul of the court, Samson, like Eulogius and Albar, began to see Cordovan Christians as divided into two camps: those who supported the martyrs and kept themselves separate from Muslims, and those who opposed the martyrs and collaborated with Muslims.

Several of the men whom Samson attacked so heatedly were bishops or former bishops. Samson, Eulogius, and Albar all agreed that the church hierarchy was guilty of collaborating with the Muslims and of failing to support the martyrs. They bemoaned the fact that church councils were largely under the government's control. Eulogius's and Albar's harshest criticisms were reserved for Reccafred, archbishop of Seville, whom Albar blamed for the mass imprisonment of clergy that occurred after Flora's arrest.[13] Eulogius seems to have viewed Reccafred's affiliation with the Muslims as a potentially contagious spiritual disease; at one point he stopped celebrating mass as a way of severing himself from the archbishop's tainted spiritual power, "lest he become entangled in [Reccafred's] error" (*ne eius gluttineratur errori*).[14]

Saul, who had the misfortune to be bishop of Córdoba during the height of the martyrs' movement, was also a target of radical Christian anger. Saul was perceived as an enemy by both the Muslim authorities and antiassimilationist Christians such as Albar. Albar described him as a traitor to the martyrs and to Christianity because of his connections with the government, whereas the government held him responsible for the martyrs' actions and imprisoned him in 851 and again in 853.[15] When the persecutions under Muhammad I began, Saul left Córdoba and went into hiding, possibly until as late as 858.[16]

During Saul's time in hiding, he and Albar carried on a lively and unfriendly correspondence, three letters of which have survived.[17] The dispute centered around Albar's having received the sacrament of penance while ill. Albar, now recovered, asks Saul in the first letter to readmit him to communion. Saul refuses, saying that Albar should have come to see him in person instead of writing and that he ought to appeal for reinstatement to the clergy who administered the sacrament in the first place. Albar, infuriated at Saul's response, lashes out at him in the last letter of the correspondence. He declares that Saul is unfit to be a bishop, accusing him of belittling the deeds of the martyrs and of abandoning his flock out of fear for his own safety. He recalls Eulogius's decision to stop saying mass so as to remove himself from the influence of Reccafred and faults Saul for forcing Eulogius to return to his priestly duties. Albar also accuses Saul of simony, saying that he paid the palace eunuchs and others four hundred solidi out of church funds for the episcopacy of Córdoba, a payment that was transacted publicly and recorded in a written statement in Arabic.

This correspondence points to some of the difficulties men in the church hierarchy faced during the time of the martyrdoms. Saul had done what was necessary to become bishop, paying fees to relevant palace officials and signing the necessary documents, all of which was probably routine; the amirs controlled episcopal appointments as an integral part of control over the Christian population. Because he was a leader of the Christian community at the time of the martyrdoms and because of the general suspicion of clergy engendered by radical Christian activity, Saul, like Abbot Samson, lost the trust of the court and was forced to flee Córdoba. The government viewed him as a troublemaker; supporters of the martyrs despised him because he was not willing to die for his faith. In another period Saul might have been a respected church official, but it is difficult to see how anyone could have been an effective bishop of Córdoba in the atmosphere of the 850s.

The Albar-Saul correspondence also indicates that the situation in Córdoba had caused serious problems of authority within the Christian church. Some letters between the two are missing, making it difficult to piece together the exact nature of the problems, but Albar and Saul seem to be arguing about a group of clergy that existed in Córdoba independent of Saul's authority. In his letter refusing to reinstate Albar to communion, Saul strongly implies that such a group existed; he says that Albar should seek dispensation from the clergy who imposed it on him in the first place and adds that he does not understand why Albar has now turned away from that group or why he calls them Migetians and Donatists (the letter in which Albar makes these statements is missing).[18] He adds that he does not see what good it will do to absolve Albar from penance today if he allies himself with a pseudo-bishop tomorrow.

One explanation of Saul's letter and Albar's use of the term "Donatists" is that there was a group of strongly antiassimilationist clergy in Córdoba who refused to accept the authority of bishops who, in their view, derived power from the Muslim government. Apparently Albar had a falling-out with this group and tried to return to Saul, who would not have him. This interpretation is supported by the fact that Eulogius had tried to remove himself from the line of sacramental authority emanating from Archbishop Reccafred. Eulogius's refusal to say mass indicates that he had taken a radical position containing echoes from the original Donatist controversy; he believed that sacramental authority could be contaminated by a bishop who colluded with the government and that such contamination could be handed down from bishop to priest. He eventually backed away from that position, but other clergy may not have done so.

The idea that a Donatist clergy existed in Córdoba is also supported by letter 10 of the Albar correspondence. The letter is unsigned but was written by a bishop; Saul is certainly a reasonable candidate for authorship.[19] The author makes two major points. In the first part of the letter he writes that a council of bishops and priests has convinced him to reconsider his decision and that he now feels that one cannot condemn those who, because of "the cruelty of these savage times," have made use of an honorable dispensation (*dispensatio honesta*). In the second half of the letter he argues against those who say that the sacraments are holy only when offered by the hands of holy men. He writes that sacraments work because the Holy Spirit mysteriously brings them to life, "nor are these gifts made greater by the merits of good dispensers, nor are they weakened by evil ones." In support of this argument he quotes extensively from Augustine and Isidore. He ends the letter by quoting Pope Celestine I to the effect that the people should be taught, not followed, and asks that if any of his congregation should complain about his new decision, his readers simply ignore them.

This letter points to two issues that were dividing the Christian community in Córdoba. First, there were those who believed it was legitimate to take advantage of a *dispensatio* and those who did not. Eulogius reports that when Muhammad I instituted new and increasingly harsh policies against Christians, many either pretended to be Muslims or actually converted to Islam; the *dispensatio* in letter 10 may have been offered later to those Christians who had denied their faith but now wished to return to the church. Albar condemns those who practice *simulatio* out of fear, by which he apparently means Christians denying their faith, or at least not advertising it.[20] The letter also makes it clear that Christians disagreed as to whether sinful clergy could legitimately administer the sacraments. These "sinful" clergymen may have been those like Reccafred or Saul, who, in the eyes of more radical Christians, had received their power from the Muslims; or they may have been priests who had taken advantage of the *dispensatio* out of fear for their safety.

If Saul wrote letter 10, he must at one time have maintained a more radical stance, condemning those who had denied their faith. His sympathy with the radical Christian stance would help explain his ill-treatment at the hands of the Muslim authorities. Later, he softened his position, a change that led to friction with radical Christians like Albar. The Donatist clergy may have established itself in response to Saul's change of heart; the author of letter 10 expects his new, more tolerant views to meet with opposition.

It is interesting that there were divisions even among the radical Christians of Córdoba. Eulogius and Albar both at one time embraced the idea of a "pure" clergy, free from the contamination of compromise with Islam, Eulogius by refusing to say mass as one of Reccafred's priests, Albar by receiving penance from a group of clergy not under Saul's control. Both backed away from that extreme position, though, and ultimately recognized Saul's authority; it was Saul who convinced Eulogius to begin saying mass again, and it was to Saul that Albar appealed for reinstatement to communion.

Splinter groups within the Christian church of al-Andalus had appeared before. Migetianism, a late eighth-century heresy originating with Migetius of Seville, was primarily a trinitarian heresy; but Migetius and his followers also reportedly refused to eat with Christians whom they regarded as sinners and taught that priests who were sinners were no longer true priests.[21] (When Albar referred to the alternative clergy in Córdoba as Migetians, he may have had their separatist attitude in mind.) A church council in Córdoba condemned a group called the Cassians or Acephali in 839. They were condemned, among other reasons, for isolating themselves from the mainstream church; they refused to eat with other Christians and would not accept penance or last rites from clergy outside their group.[22]

The Migetians and Cassians may not have directly influenced the separatist Christians in Córdoba. The Cassians apparently adhered to Jewish or Muslim food laws,[23] and they rejected the veneration of relics; their attention to food laws and their iconoclasm could have represented an attitude of accommodation rather than hostility toward Islam. The earlier existence of Migetians and Cassians shows, though, that al-Andalus already had a history of Christian splinter groups who worried about pollution from outsiders, regarding themselves as a church of the saints, believing that a sinful priest could not administer the sacraments and refusing to accept mainstream clerical authority. It was probably difficult for the church hierarchy to control such movements. Persecutions of heretics could be effective only with the secular government's support; and though Muslim rulers had a stake in supporting the authority of bishops under their control, they could not be expected to take much interest in Christians' doctrinal disputes.

The sources for ninth-century Córdoba reveal a dramatic confrontation between Christians and Muslims: Christians shouting insults against Muhammad in mosques, beheadings, bodies floating in the Guadalquivir. But a conflict that was equally bitter, if less bloody, was unfolding within the Christian community. That conflict grew out of very different ideas about the implications of being a Christian under Islamic rule.

On one side were Christians who saw Islamic rule as a fact of life which demanded compromise but did not pose any fundamental threat to Christian identity. *Dhimmi* identity created inconveniences, but one could normally conceal it or at least avoid drawing attention to it. Muslims, though a bit confused about the nature of Jesus Christ, held beliefs that were in other respects indistinguishable from those of Christians. A career at the palace required one to be circumcised and to achieve fluency in Arabic, but opportunities in government service justified making such accommodations. And if an appointment as bishop required a payment and a promise to cooperate with government policies, one could regard these as unfortunate but necessary compromises demanded of bishops since the day Constantine converted to Christianity. From this moderate point of view, Bishop Hostegesis's behavior was not out of the ordinary. He paid court officials for his office. He followed a prudent policy of ingratiating himself with the amir's sons. Given a choice between missing services for one evening or offending a powerful courtier like Hashim ibn Abd al-Aziz, he wisely chose the former. Ordering delinquent Christian taxpayers to be dragged through the streets naked may have been overzealous, but as a church official Hostegesis had to answer to the government for the conduct of those under his jurisdiction.

On the other side were radical Christians who saw Islamic rule as fundamentally incompatible with Christian life. The distance dividing the two points of view is most dramatically presented in Albar's *Indiculus luminosus*. Christians in Córdoba, according to Albar, face a disaster which many are too ignorant or complacent to see. Their Muslim rulers are more beasts than human, "gnashing their teeth and raging with wide-open dog mouths, hissing with a viper's mouth, roaring with the fierceness of lions."[24] Christians at court are no better than Muslims; one official "rose up against his own faith like a rabid dog and offered a sword to the gentiles with which to cut the throats of God's people."[25] Islam and Christianity have nothing in common. Muhammad is a precursor of the Antichrist.[26] Given these irrefutable facts, Christians must recognize that they are in immediate and great spiritual danger. They must respond by supporting the martyrs, denouncing Islam, reaffirming their own faith, and rejecting all accommodations with Muslims.

The martyrs were a natural focus of conflict between the two groups. For the radical Christians, they were heroes, people who actively preached Christianity and who recognized that the very existence of Islamic rule was a form of persecution against Christians. The martyrs were heirs to the heroic early church, ready to die for their beliefs. Their supporters were in real danger as well; Eulogius describes how the authorities burst into his home to arrest him while he was writing, disrupting his family and scattering his notes so that he feared they would be lost.[27] This group could only regard Christians who failed to support the martyrs as traitors and cowards.

More moderate Christians, for their part, saw the martyrs and their supporters as troublemakers who exaggerated the difficulties of living under Islamic rule, ruined economic and social opportunities for Christians in Córdoba, and incited the Muslims to launch a major persecution. Radical Christians, in their view, were causing an emergency, not responding to one.

Moderate members of the church hierarchy must also have recognized that radical Christians were demanding an impossible level of autonomy for the clergy, given the realities of Islamic government. Muslim rulers from the earliest days of the conquest had recognized religious groups as among the most important subdivisions of society and religious leaders as important links between the government and *dhimmi* groups. Religious leaders were spokesmen for their respective communities, and rulers governed subject communities through them. It was, therefore, highly unlikely that the amir would give up the right to have representatives present at church councils or to control the appointment of bishops.

Sources for the Cordovan Christian community of the tenth century—one hundred years after the martyrdoms—suggest that the close relationship between government and members of the church hierarchy continued. The most revealing source pertaining to Christian Córdoba in the tenth century is the *Vita Johannis abbatis Gorziensis,* which offers a vivid if limited view of the city in the 950s. The monk John of Gorze traveled to Córdoba in 953 as Otto I's envoy to Abd al-Rahman III, entrusted with delivering certain letters to the caliph. Because Muslim palace officials suspected that the letters contained insults against Islam, John and his party were detained outside the city for several years while various representatives of the palace and of the Christian church tried to persuade John to leave the letters behind when he met the caliph. John insisted that he must deliver the letters, and thus the situation stood until a compromise was reached almost three years later.

John was much impressed by the opulence of Córdoba, particularly by the luxury of the palace when he was finally allowed to go there, but he was deeply disappointed by the members of the Christian hierarchy whom he met during his stay. By this point in the tenth century the stories of the Cordovan martyrs were known in northern Europe—the tradition in the north probably began with the translation of the relics of George, Aurelius, and Sabigotho in 858—and John came to Córdoba hoping to die a glorious death as a martyr. He quickly found, however, that the important Christians in Córdoba were diplomats, not zealots, and that they wanted only to get the insulting letters away from him and thus avoid an unpleasant confrontation with the Muslims. Bishop John of Córdoba explained that the letters from Otto could endanger the whole Christian community. John of Gorze criticized the bishop for fearing conflict with the Muslims and for being lukewarm in his faith and condemned Cordovan Christians in general for practicing circumcision and conforming to Muslim food laws. Bishop John was unmoved by these criticisms; he explained that the Muslims respected good Christians and that Christians in turn were willing to cooperate with Muslims in matters that did not endanger the faith. Circumcision and compliance with food regulations were the minimal concessions that Muslims demanded of Christians with whom they had contact.

A solution was finally worked out to the problem posed by Otto's inconvenient letters: Caliph Abd al-Rahman III would send an envoy to Otto asking him to withdraw them. That task fell to Recemundus, a Christian civil servant fluent in Arabic and Latin. In exchange for his diplomatic services, Recemundus asked for gifts from the caliph, including an appointment as bishop of Granada, which Abd al-Rahman readily granted. Recemundus set out for Otto's court and returned many months later with a message from Otto withdrawing the letters. John finally visited the palace, a parade was given in his honor, and he returned home to dictate his memoirs.

Recemundus had a long and successful career in government, serving as the caliph's ambassador to the Byzantine emperor as well as to Otto.[28] He was also the author of the Calendar of Córdoba. This is a truly intercultural work, a book of days combining astronomical and agronomical information taken from Arabic sources with a Christian liturgical calendar; Recemundus presented it as a gift to al-Hakam II, Abd al-Rahman III's successor.[29] Two versions were prepared. The longer version contains the more complete liturgical calendar and seems to be intended for Christian use. The shorter edition contains less liturgical material, and the manner in which that material is abridged suggests that Recemundus presented this shorter version to the caliph. The feast days of the earliest known Cordovan martyrs, Adulphus and John, which appear in the full-length calendar, are deleted from the abridged version, as are all mentions of Paul Albar and of Speraindeo. Also missing is the festival of St. Agnes, whose bravery in the face of Roman persecution made her a model for the women martyrs of Córdoba. Recemundus also removed any mention of a later martyr, Pelagius, who was executed in 925, allegedly for refusing the sexual advances of Abd al-Rahman III.[30] There is some question as to the exact provenance of the two versions, but the evidence suggests that Recemundus intended one version for Christian consumption and the other as a gift for the caliph.[31]

Sources from the tenth century do not prove that Christian resentment of assimilation and of Muslim rule was no longer a problem in Córdoba; martyrdoms continued sporadically in the tenth century, although there is no evidence that they occurred on anything like the scale of a century earlier. It is clear, though, that the activities of radical Christians in the ninth century had had no long-term effect on the church hierarchy in Córdoba. Bishop John and Recemundus were deeply involved in court politics. Both men maintained their identities as Christians, yet as Christians at a center of Muslim power they had to present that identity in a way that did not give offense. Recemundus's two versions of the calendar—with and without martyrs—is the work of a person who has learned to negotiate between two very different worlds.

The realities of Islamic rule ultimately favored this kind of compromise. Albar's vision of a radical Christian church appealed to some Christians, but such a church could only become the focus of more violence. It could not maintain the stable relationship between government and subject population that would allow Christians to go about their daily lives in peace.

5

The Martyrs

Eulogius and Albar speak to us in their own voices. They express a wide range of discontents with Muslim rule in their attempt to justify the martyrs' movement, from personal slights they have suffered at the hands of Muslims to broader concerns about the Cordovan Christian community's loss of religious identity. The martyrs other than Eulogius probably shared many of the same concerns about the future of the Christian community and, particularly in the case of clerics and religious, suffered similar insults and humiliations. Because we know about them mostly through Eulogius's and Albar's accounts, however, it is more difficult to say exactly why they were willing to die.

Eulogius, like all of the Cordovan authors, saw events in Córdoba primarily in religious terms; it is not surprising, then, that the chief motive he attributed to the martyrs was concern about the afterlife. Some of the secret Christians, those people who would be vulnerable to charges of apostasy if they practiced Christianity openly, became afraid that their secret worship was hypocritical and that only an open profession of faith would save them from hell. Other confessors looked forward to rewards in heaven for their suffering as martyrs.

The martyrs do seem to have been people who were deeply worried about their salvation. Eulogius's descriptions of the endless fasting, praying, and weeping that formed part of many of the martyrs' personal devotion point to a sense of urgency, even of desperation, about the next life. The martyrs' detractors complained that those seeking execution were being selfish, ensuring their own place in heaven by provoking a confrontation with the Muslims, then dying and leaving the rest of the Christian community to face the consequences.[1] It has been suggested that many of the martyrs, particularly those living in monasteries, had received the sacrament of penance as a means of intensifying their asceticism and that martyrdom was a logical final expression of their penitential anxiety.[2] An explicit link between penance and martyrdom in the Iberian church goes back to Isidore of Seville, who wrote that sins can be remitted through penance just as they are through baptism and martyrdom.[3]

Beyond references to their concerns about salvation, Eulogius does not speculate much about the motives of individual martyrs. He seems to assume that the martyrdoms were the result of a natural distaste for Islam and zeal for Christianity that any good Christian should understand without explanation. As always during this tense period in Cordovan history, however, religious beliefs per se were only one element in a complex array of motives governing people's actions. Eulogius's descriptions of the martyrs' lives, careers, and families suggest a variety of reasons why people were attracted to the movement, as well as factors that helped maintain solidarity within this group of radical Christians.

One source of the movement's solidarity was its predominantly monastic character. About half of the martyrs spent at least some time in monastic communities, and Eulogius, when he first began chronicling the movement, believed that he was writing exclusively for an audience of monks and nuns.[4] The ideal Christian life which Albar and Eulogius imagined—a life defined in opposition to Islam—was most fully realized at the monasteries. Monastic life was ascetic, in contrast to the perceived decadence of the court. Monks and nuns studied Christian Scripture and thus resisted assimilation to Islamic culture.

Certain monasteries produced cohorts of martyrs. Walabonsus, his sister Maria, and Aurea all came from the convent of St. Mary. Peter, the priest who said mass as St. Mary, was also martyred. The biggest single producer of martyrs was the monastery of Tabanos; Isaac, Jeremiah, Fandila, Digna, and Columba all lived as part of that community, and Aurelius, Sabigotho, and George visited there frequently. It is no coincidence that George found his way to Tabanos immediately after he arrived in

Córdoba from North Africa. As a monk, George thought of himself as an athlete of asceticism, and he naturally gravitated toward the community best known for its own ascetic athletes and its martyrs.[5]

It is not difficult to imagine how the movement perpetuated itself within the monasteries. Monastic communities in Córdoba were small and close-knit, and members maintained an intense level of ascetic practice. This charged atmosphere nurtured the extreme feelings of penitential fervor and hostility toward Islam that inspired people to seek martyrdom, and such feelings could easily spread from person to person. Once someone from a given monastery was executed, he or she became an example to other members of the community. Some of the extremely ascetic monks and nuns who were martyred were celebrities even before they died. Habentius, and perhaps Columba, attracted sympathetic Christians from outside the monastery who came to observe their displays of asceticism.[6] If such people were famous in life, their prestige must have increased dramatically after they were martyred (and after Eulogius told their story). Such martyrs inspired other members of the community to follow them, out of religious zeal and, perhaps, a desire to share in the glory.

Just as certain monasteries produced cohorts of martyrs, certain families also became focuses of the movement; and because some of the monasteries were run by families, monastic and blood ties sometimes overlapped. Walabonsus and Maria were brother and sister. Jeremiah was Columba's brother-in-law. Aurelius, Sabigotho, Felix, and Liliosa, who died together, were all related either by blood or marriage. Aurea was the sister of John and Adulphus, who were martyred in the 820s. And Eulogius claims the martyrs Paul, Christopher, and Louis as his relatives. One execution in the family served as a model and drew other family members toward martyrdom. Family solidarity could even extend beyond death; one of the young nuns at St. Mary's had a dream in which Maria's martyred brother Walabonsus told her that Maria would soon be joining him.[7]

Eulogius and Albar themselves were a source of solidarity within the movement. Eulogius wrote his works about the martyrdoms in installments, as events progressed, and Albar wrote the *Indiculus luminosus* at the height of the movement. Eulogius in particular defined the movement and gave people a way to think about it. He shaped the stories about the martyrs, emphasizing their common goals, deemphasizing their differences, and pointing out links with the martyrs of the Roman period.

Because Eulogius intended his works primarily for a monastic audience and because many of the monks and nuns were scholars of Latin Christian literature, it seems likely that they read Eulogius's and Albar's works and that these texts were especially influential in the monasteries. By the time that Digna, who died in 853, had her vision in which the Roman martyr Agatha appeared to her and offered her a rose, a "crimson gift" representing the blood of the martyrs, Eulogius had written the first part of the *Memoriale sanctorum*, and her vision connecting her with earlier martyrs may have been shaped by his expectations.[8]

Although a disproportionate number of the martyrs came from the monasteries, the religious fervor the monastic environment in Córdoba could inspire was not the only cause of the martyrdoms. The movement quickly spread beyond the monasteries, and even those martyrs who came from monastic communities were a diverse group, ranging from people who had lived all their lives under religious vows to men who had only recently abandoned jobs with the Islamic government. Taken together, the martyrs' stories point to a variety of tensions between Muslims and Christians in Córdoba—on the streets, at the amir's court, and within mixed families. One sees in these stories a growing religious intolerance on the part of radical Christians, and some Muslims as well, and a desire to establish stronger boundaries between religious groups.

Isaac and Argimirus were the two men who had been employed at the Muslim court. Isaac had been *exceptor rei publicae* for some years before he quit his job, went into a monastery, and then three years later became the first voluntary martyr of the 850s.[9] Eulogius says that Isaac left government service because he was seized by religious fervor. This is obviously true as far as it goes: no one quits his job, becomes a monk, and then a voluntary martyr unless he has been seized by religious fervor. But it would be interesting to know more about the circumstances of Isaac's departure from office. Although Christians and Jews were employed as civil servants throughout the Islamic empire, that situation always had built-in tensions. The Quran makes it clear that Christians and Jews should not occupy positions of authority over Muslims,[10] and regulations pertaining to *dhimmi*s enforced this sense of subordination. Anyone who worked for the government was subject to the whims of the ruler—it has been suggested that government positions were readily available to *dhimmi*s because many Muslims did not want them, preferring less risky careers in business—but because of their second-class legal status, Christians and

Jews were especially vulnerable to attack.[11] It is therefore possible that Isaac was driven out of the government by anti-Christian prejudice. His rank was the same as that held some time later by the Christian courtier Ibn Antonian; Christians like Ibn Antonian could attain high positions in government in this period, but above a certain level Muslims' negative feelings about Christians in power tended to surface. If Isaac was the victim of such prejudice, then his ultimately suicidal confrontation with the *qadi* may have contained an element of revenge against those who had forced him out of office. Though powerless, he could still insult and defy them.

It is also possible that Eulogius's assessment of the situation is correct and that Isaac left government voluntarily, out of concern for his spiritual well-being. His sudden move into a monastic community and subsequent martyrdom would then represent a decision to break all ties with Islamic culture and reestablish himself as a Christian. Monastic life could also have been tied to penance, a desire to atone for all his years of working for the Muslims. Or all these factors may have played a role and reinforced each other; perhaps his becoming a more devout Christian made him unpopular at court, and becoming unpopular at court made him a more radical Christian. That dynamic seems to have been at work in the case of Abbot Samson.

Argimirus was an older man who had worked in the government for many years and then retired into a monastery.[12] In 856, some years after his retirement, his Muslim former colleagues denounced him before the *qadi,* saying that he had made insulting remarks about the Prophet. Argimirus was arrested and, when he did not deny the charges, was executed. Eulogius gives us few details about the situation, but clearly, as in Isaac's case, a man who had made a career for himself in the Islamic government had become a radical opponent of Islam, and Muslims who had once been his colleagues had become his enemies. Again, it would be interesting to know precisely what led to this estrangement: whether Argimirus left the government out of religious zeal, because he was forced out, or because of some combination of factors.

The stories of Isaac and Argimirus highlight how difficult it is to know whether the hostilities at court originated with Christians or Muslims. I would suggest that by the 850s, as Islamic culture at court became increasingly well-defined, two related developments occurred: Christians in the civil service were less welcome, and Christians in general had more incentive to convert to Islam. Many did convert, or at least stopped specifically identifying themselves as Christians. Many did not, however, and they felt themselves to be increasingly pushed to the margins of Cordovan society. This sense of being pushed aside fed anti-Islamic feelings and led to public demonstrations against Islam, which in turn led to worse treatment of Christians.

Again, some interesting parallels can be made between events in ninth-century Córdoba and Syria at the time of John of Damascus. In the first half of the eighth century, barriers preventing the conversion of *dhimmi*s to Islam began to collapse, while at the same time *dhimmi*s at court who did not convert were viewed with increasing suspicion.[13] These changes in government alone do not explain the no doubt complex personal reasons for John's conversion to monastic life, but they do suggest that certain changes in Islamic society can provide a background for the religious fervor of the sort demonstrated by Isaac and Argimirus.

Another group of biographical sketches revealing tensions between Muslims and Christians are those pertaining to the martyrs raised in religiously mixed families. A substantial number of the martyrs—at least twelve—came from such families. Nunilo and Alodia, Flora, and Aurelius were born to Muslim fathers and Christian mothers, which is the pattern one would anticipate because Islamic law allows Muslim men to marry *dhimmi* women but not the other way around. Some of the other families, however, did not follow this expected pattern. Some families seem to have been almost exclusively Muslim with a few stray Christian members and to have had a strong sense of Muslim identity. Others had Christian or at least secret Christian members and a less decidedly Muslim identity. On one extreme, for example, Albar characterizes Leocritja's family as predominantly Muslim, saying that she was born "out of the filth of the gentiles"; she did have a relative who was a Christian nun, but both of her parents were Muslims, and for her to profess Christianity was a clear act of apostasy.[14] The martyr Rudericus was a priest and had one Christian brother and one Muslim brother.[15] Such a family, in which two of the men could live openly as Christians, had a less decidedly Muslim religious identity; Rudericus's brother could make a charge of apostasy against him credible only by claiming that he had converted to Islam, then recanted.

Two types of scenarios led to the execution of members of such families as apostates. In some cases it was the Christian family members who provoked the crisis. Some of the martyrs had kept their religion a secret from the Muslims in the family and then suddenly and dramatically revealed their Christianity in public; Aurelius, Sabigotho, Felix, and Liliosa brought about their own arrest by openly attending church.[16] Other mixed families tolerated Christians in the family for years, particularly if they were women. Because women were not active in public life, Muslim family members may not have cared much that they were Christians so long as they were discreet about it and did not become a source of public ridicule. The situation changed, however, when women became more open about their beliefs. Nunilo and Alodia elaborated their ascetic practices until they became objects of public discussion;[17] Flora ran away from home and defied her brother's authority in public;[18] Leocritja, to intensify her Christian devotion, refused to attend parties or dress in attractive clothing and eventually ran away from home. Those women became embarrassments to their families. Once that line was crossed, their families would no longer protect them from charges of apostasy and often brought the charges themselves.

All of the Christians who precipitated crises within their families preferred to die rather than continue to keep their beliefs private. Their intense desire to practice their religion publicly echoes one of Albar's complaints about Christian life in Córdoba, that the worst sort of persecution is that which prohibits one from speaking freely what is in his heart.[19] Apparently some Christians in the 850s agreed with Albar and were willing to die because of their belief that Christianity was not just something one felt inwardly but a complete way of living one's life which must be expressed publicly as well as privately.

In most instances, the martyrs from religiously mixed families deliberately defied and provoked their Muslim relatives. In two cases, however, Muslims in the family precipitated the crisis. The priest Rudericus's Muslim brother went to great lengths to incriminate him. He falsely told the community that Rudericus had converted to Islam, then had him arrested as an apostate the next time he appeared in priest's robes. Aurea was a Christian nun from, according to Eulogius, a noble Arab family, which included the *qadi* of Córdoba among its members.[20] Having a Christian nun for a relative must have been an embarrassment to such a family. Aurea had, however, been a nun for thirty years before her family sought

her arrest, and there is no evidence that she was more of an embarrassment in 856 than she had been thirty years earlier. Also, the members of
her family who demanded her arrest lived in Seville, not Córdoba, which
suggests that they went out of their way to cause trouble for her.

The martyrs' movement itself may have accounted for some of this
Muslim intolerance. Aurea was executed in 856, Rudericus in 857, when
the movement was well under way. By that point the amir had moved
to suppress Christian dissent, and relations between the two religious
groups had grown extremely tense so that Muslims who might in the
past have felt resentment toward Christian relatives now acted on their
feelings. Rudericus's brother accused him of apostasy, knowing that the
penalty would be death; Flora's brother had her beaten; Leocritja's family
sent the authorities after her, aware that they could well execute her if
they found her.

A disproportionate number of the martyrs from mixed families were
women. Counting Eulogius, there were fifty martyrs in the 850s. Out of
those, twelve were women. Of the twelve martyrs who we are reasonably sure came from mixed families, eight were women, leaving only four
women martyrs who are not known to be from such a background.

The close connection between religious conflicts and family tensions
is particularly striking in the case of the women martyrs, whether from a
mixed family or not. A number of the women martyrs used their religious
enthusiasm as a means of defying their families' authority; Columba, for
example, wanted to enter a monastery partly to avoid the marriage her
mother had arranged for her.[21] Being a part of the monastic and ascetic
milieu surrounding the martyrs' movement gave women opportunities
they would not otherwise have had. Eulogius notes that several of the
women were accomplished scriptural scholars, most notably Columba.
Some of the women martyrs became local celebrities because of their ascetic practices; it was such notoriety that eventually led to Nunilo and
Alodia's arrest. The fact of being martyred itself gave women a chance to
show a level of courage and strength normally associated only with men.

Such opportunities may have been even more important to women
from Muslim families, who would have had even less of a public role as
married women than their counterparts from wholly Christian families.
Islam, moreover, did not offer an institutional alternative to marriage as
did Christian monasticism. Aurea and her mother, Artemia, presided over

a monastic community and controlled their own affairs for thirty years as Christian nuns; they could not have achieved so much independence as Muslim women in a prominent Arab family.

Christianity offered a young woman from a mixed family a dramatic way to defy her relatives. Leocritja's vigils and fasting, not to mention her running away to live among Christians, effectively disrupted her parents' household. Her insistence on maintaining her ascetic practices resulted in a prolonged struggle for power with her parents, not unlike modern-day struggles between anorexic girls and their families.[22] The first time Flora ran away from home, she did not go directly to the home of her Christian sister in Martos to begin enjoying life in a Christian household; she could not resist going home first to confront her Muslim brother, even though she must have known how dangerous this was.

Eulogius recognized women as important contributors to the radical Christian movement, and he played a role in attracting them to the movement.[23] He took women seriously as scholars and as ascetics, admired their courage, and devoted a great deal of space to them in his writings. He also realized that he could use women to further his objectives. The Muslims were interested in men. There were subtle and not so subtle pressures on men to convert to Islam and rewards for them if they did so. There was far less pressure on women, however, and many Muslims seemed willing to tolerate Christian women in the family so long as they practiced their religion privately. Eulogius was, as it were, working the other side of the street. Partly through his efforts, two women from important and largely Muslim families—Flora and Leocritja—publicly turned against Islam. Eulogius may have hoped that through such women, the tide of conversion and assimilation to Islam could be turned back.

Although the martyrs' movement drew much of its support from a limited number of monasteries and families, it would be a mistake to see the martyrs as a homogeneous group. There were as many motives for their involvement in this radical Christian movement as there were martyrs. They were worried about their salvation; they were angry at their employers; they wanted to practice their religion openly; they longed to be free of their parents' authority.

Some of the martyrs had lived their adult lives in monasteries isolated from Islamic culture. Many, though, were intimately associated with Muslims or had at one time been Muslim themselves. In fact, tensions between Christians and Muslims in ninth-century Córdoba were particu-

larly violent in situations that required Christians and Muslims to associate closely: at court and in mixed families. Córdoba in the mid-ninth
century was a place where Christians and Muslims lived and worked
together and where Christians were becoming increasingly assimilated
to Islamic culture. The evidence provided by the martyrs' biographies,
though, shows that people were not always comfortable with that situation; some Christians reacted to assimilation and conversion by defining
themselves more completely and publicly as Christians, while some Muslims turned against Christian colleagues and family members. Tensions
between the two groups were just under the surface, and in the 850s they
exploded in a crisis during which one colleague might accuse another of
capital crimes and men wished their sisters and daughters dead.

6

Problems of Religious and Cultural Identity

Much has been said up to this point about Christians converting and assimilating in ninth-century Córdoba, but we have
not yet examined the question of what people were converting or assimilating from or to. In Córdoba, where Christians and Muslims
might intermarry, where a person might be a Muslim in public and a
Christian at home, and where some people saw few important theological differences between the two religions, what exactly did it mean to be
a Christian or a Muslim? What mixture of belief, behavior, education, or
heredity defined those categories?

One way to approach these questions is to focus on the meaning of
religious conversion for people in Islamic Córdoba and to recognize that
they thought of it as a social more than an individual transformation. St.
Augustine's conversion as he describes it in the *Confessions* fits a model of
religious affiliation that makes sense to twentieth-century readers in that
his conversion was primarily a personal matter. It was motivated by his
particular family history and emotional makeup and by his intellectual
and spiritual quest for meaning. The transformation he underwent was
primarily internal, a shift in the way he understood the meaning of his
life.[1] The conversion of the Germanic tribal leader Clovis to Christianity,
however, followed a different pattern. A personal spiritual quest in that
case was secondary; Clovis's main goal was to ally himself and his people
with the Gallo-Roman aristocracy and with the prestigious political and

cultural tradition of the Roman Empire. His conversion may strike us as hypocritical, as "not real," because it did not primarily represent a transformation of the inner self; it represented a shift to a new cultural and social identity. It was as much a conversion to *romanitas* as to Christianity.

The gradual process by which peoples of the Middle East and al-Andalus converted to Islam in the centuries after the Arab conquests has more in common with Clovis's conversion than with Augustine's. This is not to say that individual spiritual and emotional needs played no role in these conversions. Along with whatever internal shifts in perception accompanied conversion, however, a change in religious affiliation involved practical changes in people's social ties and cultural practices. Religious communities were among the most important subgroups within Islamic societies in this period; membership in a community defined one's legal status, tax obligations, marriage opportunities, and to some extent the body of linguistic and cultural skills one would be expected to possess. A convert exchanged one community for another. When Albar complained about losing young men to Islam, he was not only talking about their souls but about losing them to a whole new set of friends and colleagues and interests.[2]

Defining precisely what this shift between communities entailed is complicated for two reasons. First, conversion to Islam in ninth-century Córdoba was a process rather than an event. There was a moment at which one ceased to be a Christian and began to be a Muslim by passing through a formal ritual of conversion; in the case of Islam this meant the reciting before witnesses of the *shahada*, Islam's most basic profession of belief in a single god and in the prophecy of Muhammad: "There is no God but God and Muhammad is his prophet." Although both Latin and Arabic sources recognize the importance of such a defining moment, neither side focuses on conversion as a single act. Authors of both faiths are more interested in the whole constellation of attitudes and practices that Christian and formerly Christian men had to adopt to be successful at the Islamic court. Because conversion could be a gradual taking on of a Muslim identity, it was difficult to say exactly when a man stopped being a Christian and began to be a Muslim. Radical Christians like Eulogius and Albar saw almost any accommodation with Muslim practice as a serious sin bordering on apostasy; other Christians were more flexible in their thinking.

The second complicating factor was a disagreement within both groups as to the exact nature of Muslim or Christian identity. Radical Christians, and some Arab Muslims as well, saw culture and language as important aspects of religious identity: a good Christian studied Latin literature, while a good Muslim was fluent in Arabic. Other Christians and Muslims attached less importance to cultural characteristics. A convert was clearly moving from one community to another, yet neither community had fully worked out its qualifications for membership; and because the shift could be gradual, it was difficult to say at what point the convert had arrived.

Islam, like Judaism, centers around an extensive law code (the *sharia*), which regulates many aspects of the believer's life. Christians who converted to Islam were, of course, expected to adopt all aspects of Islamic practice. Even men who remained Christian, however, could not hope for serious advancement at the Islamic court unless they followed enough of the *sharia* to avoid giving offense to Muslims. Muslims were particularly sensitive about violations of food and hygiene laws. Abbot Samson and John of Gorze both report that Muslims at the palace refused to work with men who did not respect Muslim food restriction or who were uncircumcised. The fact that a man was a Christian was not necessarily a problem for Muslims, but a Christian who was physically polluted by eating pork or by not being circumcised was intolerable. Christians who opposed assimilation focused on the issue of circumcision as much as Muslims did and were deeply offended by Christians who made this concession to Islamic culture, as Samson's graphic account of Avurnus's circumcision testifies. Samson's account suggests the almost physical loathing he felt for Muslims and assimilated Christians.

This preoccupation with circumcision is interesting in that circumcision is not a major issue in the scripture of either Christianity or Islam. New Testament references to circumcision occur in Paul's letters, and although Paul considers circumcision to be unnecessary, he does not forbid it.[3] Circumcision receives correspondingly scant attention in Islamic scripture. The Quran does not mention it at all, while the *hadith* refer to it only briefly as a desirable practice, along with keeping one's nails trimmed.[4] Cordovan Muslims appear to have passed over other, more basic aspects of Islamic law; Quran and *hadith* strictly and repeatedly forbid the consumption of alcohol, for example, yet there is no evidence that any person was ever dismissed from the court for drunkenness.[5] Circumcision may have seemed particularly important in a pluralistic society like that of Córdoba because it created a visible and permanent mark on the body showing one's cultural identity.

The men who worked with a Christian courtier knew that he was a Christian, no matter how meticulously he followed certain Muslim practices. In the context of more casual social contacts, however, many Christians in Córdoba passed as Muslims. Such passing took different forms. In some cases, Christians did not actually claim to be Muslims but dressed and behaved in such a way that they could not be readily identified as *dhimmi*s. A different form of passing was practiced by Christians who were children of mixed marriages and were thus obliged to keep their religious beliefs secret.

Christians in ninth-century Córdoba disagreed about the morality of such accommodations with Islamic culture. Most Christians seem to have regarded some degree of cultural accommodation as acceptable. Others, however—notably those who became martyrs or were associated with them—saw the practices of passing for Muslim or conforming to Islamic law as deeply significant, perhaps even as acts of apostasy. At the base of these differing opinions lay fundamental questions about what it meant to be a Christian. If a man became circumcised, kept Islamic food laws, and worked among Muslims all day, being careful not to give offense or mention his own religious views, was he still a Christian? What if he allowed customers and casual acquaintances to believe he was a Muslim? Finally, what about the man who actively declared to the world that he was a Muslim yet in his heart thought of himself as a Christian? In what sense was he a Christian?

Questions about the relationship between one's public and private religious identity may have arisen for Christians partly because of their perceptions of Islam. The Islam that Christians saw in Córdoba was a religion of public life, of the court. It was the set of cultural and social skills that one needed to be successful. On the one hand, radical Christians criticized what they perceived as the outwardness of Islam, arguing that it was nothing but a collection of superficial rules about the body having nothing to do with the inner person. On the other hand, the public nature of Islam in Córdoba prompted Christians to think about their own religion in the same terms. Perhaps Christianity could not be defined by purely private, even secret worship. Perhaps it needed to be part of the believer's public life as well, as Islam was for the Muslim believer.

Passing and conforming to Islamic law were forms of accommodation with Islamic culture that were of particular concern to radical Christians. Another form of accommodation that raised issues of religious identity for both Christians and Muslims was the adoption of specifically Arab culture, as opposed to Islamic practice, by Christians and former Christians. Both groups struggled with the question of how closely the religion òf Islam was connected with Arab language and culture: could someone who studied Arabic letters be a good Christian? Could someone who was ignorant of Arabic letters be a good Muslim?

One of the major indicators of status at court was the extent to which one could claim to be Arab. Being Arab in ninth-century Córdoba was partly a question of blood, meaning that people who could trace their lineage back to aristocratic Arab families enjoyed a certain social precedence. This concept of blood was, however, quite different from a modern racial theory in two respects. First, chiefly the father's blood was important, so that the amir Abd al-Rahman II could marry a Basque wife but still feel confident that his children would be Arab.[6] Second, it was seen as theoretically possible to acquire a new *nasab,* or genealogy. Al-Jahiz, a scholar at the Abbasid court whose works were known in Córdoba, suggests that a client or *mawla* of an Arab tribe could eventually acquire his patron's *nasab.*[7] Genealogy was important, but it was interpreted in a fairly flexible way. It was also recognized that good blood alone did not guarantee personal excellence. The courtier Hashim ibn Abd al-Aziz was extremely proud of his Arab lineage; but when a visiting scholar wishes to praise Hashim, he mentions not only his paternity (*ubuwwah*) but also his personal worth and power (*qadar*).[8]

Although genealogy was an important factor in determining who was an Arab and who was not, behavior and education were at least as important. High status at court was linked to one's ability to speak and write Arabic well and to a knowledge of Arabic literature, both sacred and secular.

Skill in Arabic language and letters did not always follow religious or ethnic lines. Not all Muslims knew Arabic well. Arab Muslims who came from particularly old and respected families made a point of speaking only Arabic, but these aristocratic Arabs never constituted more than a small minority within the Muslim population of al-Andalus. Much of the original invading force had been made up of Berbers, whose first language was not Arabic, and of course native Iberians who converted after the invasion were also non-Arabic-speakers. One Arabic chronicle commends an Iberian Muslim religious leader as a fine, devout Muslim but ridicules his inability to employ the Arabic definite article correctly, a common problem for those who learn Arabic as a second language.[9] But one did not need to be either a Muslim or an Arab by blood to be skilled at Arabic letters; both the Latin and Arabic sources mention *dhimmi*s and converts at court who were celebrated for their linguistic abilities.[10] Any young man who wanted a career in government, regardless of his religious or ethnic background, was well advised to begin studying Arabic at a young age.

Radical Christians recognized the importance of linguistic skills in a pluralistic environment like that of Córdoba—Eulogius wrote admiringly of Perfectus's and Isaac's command of Arabic—but they condemned Christians who abandoned the study of Latin in favor of Arabic, just as they condemned those who adopted Muslim practices. Eulogius and Albar were concerned not only that Christians would abandon their religion but that they would reject the entire Western, Latin literary tradition in favor of Arabic letters.

Their concern about the fate of Latin letters was justified. Descendants of the original invaders, especially those who intermarried with native Iberian families, adopted Romance as the informal spoken language of the home and the marketplace, and Romance was also the first spoken language of Iberian converts to Islam.[11] Latin, however, was never adopted as a vehicle of Islamic thought. The linguistic situation of al-Andalus was therefore quite different than that of Persia, where the Arab invaders also encountered an ancient literary tradition. Arabic was the dominant language of high culture throughout the Umayyad and Abbasid periods, but by the eighth century, Persian poetry, fables, and treatises on government were being translated into Arabic and strongly influenced Abbasid court literature. After the collapse of Abbasid power in the tenth century, an Arabic-influenced form of the Persian language became a vehicle for Islamic culture, both religious and secular.[12] This adaptation of the indigenous literary tradition to Islamic needs never took place in al-Andalus. Latin letters at the time of the Muslim invasion were too restricted to purely Christian uses to be of much interest to Muslims.[13] In addition, Arabic high culture in al-Andalus was modeled largely on that of the Abbasid Empire and was therefore not open to influence from Latin high culture.[14] In Persia, the population's conversion to Islam did not mean the end of the indigenous high cultural tradition. In al-Andalus, it did. For

Christians who knew and cared about the Latin literary tradition, language became a symbol of cultural loyalty, much like circumcision. A true Christian studied Latin; a man who studied Arabic exclusively had gone over to the enemy. For the radical minority of Christians associated with the martyrs' movement, religion and culture in a broader sense must be congruent: a man could not abandon Latin letters and still be a good Christian.

For other Cordovan Christians, however, and for the Muslims, the relationship between cultural and religious identity was less clear. For Muslims, being an Arab and being a good Muslim were in a sense separate issues. Muhammad may have imagined a religion chiefly for Arabs, but that understanding of Islam had broken down long before the 850s; a *muwallad* could be described as a pious Muslim. Nevertheless, at the very highest levels of power in Cordovan society, Arab blood, Arab culture, and Muslim identity were interrelated.

The complexities of these issues are illustrated by the career of Amr ibn Abd Allah, who during the reign of the amir Muhammad I (852–86) twice held the position of *qadi*.[15] Amr was from an Iberian Muslim family and was, according to one source the first *muwallad* to hold the office of *qadi*.[16] Both terms ended when he was deposed from office, the first time because he ruled against the interests of the powerful courtier Hashim ibn Abd al-Aziz, the second time for theft and accepting bribes.[17] Long before any rumors of graft or theft emerged, however, Amr's appointment was opposed by Córdoba's prominent Arab families, who were uncomfortable with the idea of a non-Arab *qadi*. Many said that it was acceptable for him to carry out his legal duties as *qadi*—which consisted of settling legal disputes on the basis of *sharia*—but that they did not believe he was qualified to lead the community in prayer during Friday services at the mosque.

Until Amr was charged with various unethical activities late in his second term, everyone seemed to believe that he was a devout Muslim and an expert in Islamic jurisprudence. Yet he was not a proper Muslim in Arab eyes, not the sort of person who should be entrusted with the community's spiritual well-being. Behind the spiritual question may lie a social issue. At Friday prayer, the *qadi* acts as the *imam,* that is, as the person whose position is at the head of the congregation and who acts as a model for the other believers to follow in prayer. The Arabs voiced their objections to Amr's role as leader of prayer by saying, "We will not pray behind him."[18] They found it socially embarrassing to pray behind and thus show deference to a non-Arab in a public setting. This sense on the part of the Arab elite that Amr was not really one of them probably contributed to his downfall as much as did any criminal charges or conflicts with courtiers.

Ambiguities of culture, religion, and blood are illustrated most dramatically by the career of a civil servant at Córdoba known in the Arabic sources as Qumis Ibn Antonian.[19] Ibn Antonian was a Christian who converted to Islam and an Iberian who identified himself completely with Arab culture. His career demonstrates both the extent to which a talented and ambitious man could manipulate his cultural identity in ninth-century Córdoba and the limitations of such manipulation.

Ibn Antonian is mentioned in several Arabic sources and is probably the *exceptor rei publicae* whom Eulogius so despised, although Eulogius does not tell us his name. Still a Christian when he entered government service, he quickly rose to a high position. The sources agree that his swift promotion was a result of his intelligence and his linguistic abilities. He was renowned for his elegant style in both written and spoken Arabic, and he also knew Latin well enough to act as the Muslim government's correspondent with European princes.[20] During the reign of Muhammad I, he converted to Islam. According to the Arabic sources, he converted because the amir made it known that he favored Ibn Antonian for the office of chief administrator (*al-katib al-azim*) but was not willing to promote a *dhimmi* to such a high position. According to a Latin source, he converted at the height of the martyrs' movement because Muhammad I indicated that he would no longer tolerate *dhimmi*s at court.[21] Whatever his reasons, Ibn Antonian converted to Islam and was made head of the Umayyad bureaucracy.

The degree of Ibn Antonian's assimilation to Arab culture is illustrated by the way he is described in the Arabic chronicles. The chronicler al-Khushani generally used the word *ajami* to refer to a Christian. *Ajami* was, strictly speaking, a broad cultural designation rather than a religious designation; it meant someone who was not an Arabic speaker and, by extension, someone who was not culturally an Arab. In the eastern Islamic lands it denoted a Persian-speaker, and in al-Andalus a speaker of Romance. Even when referring to the time before his conversion, however, al-Khushani never described Ibn Antonian as an *ajami* but always as a *nasrani*, a Nazarene. He was a Christian but could not be labeled as a non-Arabic-speaker.

Up to this point, Ibn Antonian's conversion had gone smoothly. He was no doubt circumcised and willing to conform to relevant aspects of Islamic practice even before his formal conversion. He had mastered Arabic and other aspects of Arab culture. When pressed by circumstances, he finalized the process of conversion with a formal profession of Islam. This conversion led to a high position in the Islamic government.

As soon as he became chief administrator, however, Ibn Antonian became the object of considerable suspicion. Two accusations were leveled against him: that he was not really an Arab and that he was not really a Muslim. The same Hashim who caused so many problems for Amr ibn Abd-Allah attempted to discredit Ibn Antonian. Hashim was extremely proud of his Arab lineage and was deeply offended that a non-Arab should hold such a high position (the two men also disagreed about policy). Ibn al-Qutiyya reports that Hashim felt choked by Ibn Antonian, as though he had a bone caught in his throat.[22] Finally, Hashim complained to Muhammad I that it was unseemly for a non-Arab to hold such an important post, asking him what the Abbasids would think when they heard that the amir had appointed a Christian to the highest secretariat. (Bringing up the Abbasids was a shrewd tactic in that Muhammad I, like other leaders of al-Andalus, probably feared being seen as provincial by the caliph in Baghdad.) His characterization of Ibn Antonian as a Christian even after his conversion suggests that for Hashim at least, a convert was not a real Muslim, or at least not real enough to be in a position of power.[23]

Other courtiers also complained that Ibn Antonian's conversion had been a ruse and that he continued to practice Christianity in secret. The amir eventually dismissed him on the basis of such accusations. Even after Ibn Antonian died, Hashim sought to discredit his former colleague. He found numerous witnesses who testified that Ibn Antonian had died professing Christianity, which would have made him an apostate and caused his property to go to the state treasury rather than to his family. Hashim's position was clear: Arab culture and Arab blood were integral parts of being a good Muslim.

Ibn Antonian's career suggests that a Christian or former Christian could rise to a certain status within the Islamic power structure without undue problems, provided his Arabic and his social skills were of high quality. Above a certain level, though, being a non-Arab and a recent convert could become heavy liabilities. Not everyone agreed with Hashim's inflexible position, however, and Ibn Antonian continued to enjoy some support among the Cordovan elite even after he was dismissed. Many courtiers disliked Hashim and saw him as an opportunist who wanted the position of chief administrator for himself; for every witness Hashim produced saying that Ibn Antonian died a Christian, another would testify that he was a devout Muslim, testimony which ultimately led the *qadi* to allow the family to inherit.[24] Muslims, like Christians, seem to have held a variety of opinions about the relationship between religion, culture, and blood.

The careers of Ibn Antonian and Amr ibn Abd-Allah raised troubling questions for Muslims. Were converts equal to other Muslims? Could they hold positions of authority? What constituted a true conversion? Was Ibn Antonian's conversion too closely tied to his political ambitions, even for the practical, career-oriented Umayyad court? What made a man an Arab? Was it a question of cultural literacy, or blood, or both? Were Arabs better Muslims than non-Arabs? Were Arabs uniquely qualified for positions of authority?

The legal status of converts was clarified early in the history of Islam. In the seventh century, Arab rulers attempted to maintain the link between Arab and Muslim identity. To convert to Islam, a non-Arab had to become the client, or *mawla,* of an Arab tribe, a position that implied second-class status. By the early decades of the eighth century, however, this situation had begun to change, and under the rule of the Umayyad caliph Umar II, non-Arab Muslims were granted a legal and fiscal status more or less equal to that of Arab Muslims.[25] The goal of equality for converts was furthered when the Abbasids overthrew the Umayyads in 750. Because their core of support lay in Khurasan, among converts and among Arab Muslims who had assimilated to the local culture, the Abbasids promoted the ideal of an empire based on allegiance to Islam, not on Arab ethnicity.[26]

Questions about Arab supremacy in government and society were not entirely laid to rest by these legal decrees, however, or by the Abbasid revolution. The Umayyad caliphs gave Islamic government a decidedly Arab stamp, for example, by promoting Arabic as the exclusive language of government;[27] and despite Abbasid policy favoring equality among all believers, Arabic continued to be the language of government and culture at the Abbasid court. In the long run, the spread of Islam to non-Arab peoples made it inevitable that Muslim identity would cease to be equated with Arab identity. After the collapse of Abbasid power in the tenth century, Persian became an acceptable vehicle of Islamic culture; with the Turkish invasions of the tenth and eleventh centuries the tradition of Arab dominance in government ended.[28] In the ninth century, though, these issues were not completely settled.

They were probably farther from being settled in al-Andalus than in the Abbasid empire. Spain did not have as widespread and entrenched an indigenous high culture as that of Persia so that a challenge to Arab cultural supremacy was less feasible. Furthermore, there was no Abbasid revolution in al-Andalus. The Umayyads came to power in al-Andalus on the basis of aristocratic Arab support and thus had less reason than the Abbasids to promote an ideal of equality among all believers. Finally, al-Andalus, despite the amirs' efforts to import culture, was still the provinces. Cordovans were the last to learn how to arrange their hair in the Baghdadi fashion, and they also lagged behind in their efforts to settle difficult questions of cultural and religious identity.

Christians in Córdoba were going through much the same process of questioning, which produced a similar range of opinion. Many Christians saw no necessary link between culture and religion; radical Christians did. Eulogius and Albar did not seem to view lineage as a determining factor in religious identity—a Christian with Muslim parents is as good a Christian as any other—but they had much in common with Hashim in seeing a strong connection between cultural identity and religion.

Conversion to Islam in ninth-century Córdoba and the tensions that accompanied it can be understood as part of a process that was taking place throughout the Islamic world: as the rulers of a multicultural empire, Muslims were struggling to define what it meant to be a Muslim and to determine what the roles of Arab Muslims, converts, and *dhimmis* ought to be in an Islamic society. At the same time, certain characteristics specific to ninth-century al-Andalus—in particular the insecure position of Latin high culture and the continued high status attached to being an Arab—help account for the confusion, discomfort, and anger that Muslims and Christians alike clearly felt when faced with questions of cultural and religious identity.

Notes

Introduction

1. The sources do not describe the exact setting of most executions, but they do make it clear that the beheadings were public spectacles. See in particular Aimoin, *De translatione*, 3.28.

2. Eulogius's main works concerning the martyrs are the *Documentum martyriale*, the *Liber apologeticus martyrum*, and the *Memoriale sanctorum*.

3. The *Indiculus luminosus* and the *Vita Eulogii*.

4. This view of the Islamic period informs the argument of Sánchez Albornoz in his *España, un enigma histórico*.

5. Isidro de las Cagigas treats Christian subject communities as early centers of Spanish nationalism in his *Los mozárabes*.

6. This view is forcefully expressed by Simonet in *Historia de los mozárabes*. In spite of the outdated interpretive framework, the basic research of this book is still valuable. Simonet's most interesting work explores language usage in Islamic Spain; see his *Glosario de voces ibéricas y latinas usadas entre los mozárabes*.

7. Reinhardt Dozy in his *Histoire des musulmans d'Espagne* is particularly dismissive of Christian culture. Evariste Lévi-Provençal is more sympathetic to Christians under Islam but still minimizes the significance of the martyrs; see his *Histoire de l'Espagne musulmane*, 1:226–27.

8. Thomas Glick examines Christian and Muslim culture without romanticizing either one in *Islamic and Christian Spain in the Early Middle Ages*. Glick

works in the tradition of the best of the Spanish scholars, particularly Américo Castro.

9. The most important exception is Waltz, "The Significance of the Voluntary Martyrs of Ninth-Century Córdoba." Waltz places the movement in the context of shifts in both the Islamic world and the Christian West.

10. Bernard Lewis explores the reality and the limitations of medieval Islam's tolerance in *The Jews of Islam*, 3–66.

11. In particular, by their contemporary in Córdoba, Abbot Samson, who wrote the *Apologeticus* in the 860s and, from the tenth century, Abbot John of St. Arnulf, *Vita Johannis abbatis Gorziensis*.

12. Arabic sources relevant to the study of ninth-century Cordovan society include Ibn Hayyan, *Al-Muqtabas min anba ahl al-Andalus*; Ibn Hazm, *Jamharat ansab al-Arab*; Ibn al-Qutiyya, *Tarikh iftitah al-Andalus*; al-Khushani, *Kitab al-qudat bi Qurtuba*; and al-Maqqari, *Nafh al-tib*.

13. The best attempt to do so is Wolf, *Christian Martyrs*. Wolf depicts Eulogius's interests and motives as quite different from those of the other martyrs.

1. The Islamic Background

1. For a narrative of the Arab conquests, see (among many others) Shaban, *Islamic History*; Wellhausen, *The Arab Kingdom and Its Fall*; and al-Baladhuri, *Origins of the Islamic State*.

2. For discussions of *dhimmi* status see Lewis, *Jews of Islam*, 3–66; Schacht, *Introduction to Islamic Law*, 130–33; Tritton, *The Caliphs and Their Non-Muslim Subjects*; and Ye'or, *The Dhimmi*.

3. Simonet, *Historia de los mozárabes*, 106–7.

4. Goitein, *Mediterranean Society*, 2:2–3.

5. Shaban, *Islamic History*, 165–89, describes this process of demilitarization. Also see Lapidus, *History of Islamic Societies*, 45–53.

6. Collins, *The Arab Conquest of Spain*, 42–44. Wolf, *Christian Martyrs*, 9, suggests that this was the case because al-Andalus was conquered relatively late, after the rules of the *dhimma* had evolved to replace physical separation with legal separation.

7. In particular see Grabar, *Formation of Islamic Art*, and Hodgson, *Venture of Islam*, 1:410–72.

8. See Glick and Pi-Sunyer, "Acculturation as an Explanatory Concept in Spanish History," for a more technical discussion of acculturation theory.

9. For a discussion of the distinction between acculturation and assimilation, see Broom et al., "Acculturation."

10. See Lévi-Provençal, *Histoire de l'Espagne musulmane*, 1:8–30, for a narrative and a list of sources pertaining to the Muslim invasion of Spain.

11. Barbero and Vigil, *Sobre los orígenes sociales de la Reconquista*, 13–106.

12. Ziegler, *Church and State in Visigothic Spain*, 136–99.

13. Lévi-Provençal, *Histoire de l'Espagne musulmane*, 1:83–89. But see also Taha, *Muslim Conquest*, 234–53. According to Taha, many of the Umayyad family's clients (*mawali*) were Berber and accompanied Abd al-Rahman to Córdoba.

14. Lévi-Provençal, *Histoire de l'Espagne musulmane*, 1:41–44.

15. Shaban, *Islamic History*, 34–59, 120–26.

16. Lévi-Provençal, *Histoire de l'Espagne musulmane*, 1:44–51.

17. See Shaban, *Abbasid Revolution*, 138–68, and Hodgson, *Venture of Islam*, 1:241–79.

18. Lévi-Provençal, *Histoire de l'Espagne musulmane*, 1:91–104.

19. Ibid., 240–73.

20. Shaban, *Islamic History*, 31–35.

21. al-Maqqari, *Nafh al-tib*, 3:122–33.

22. Eulogius, *Memoriale*, 2.1.1, translation by Colbert, *Martyrs of Córdoba*, 194.

23. Albar, *Indiculus*, 35, translation by Colbert, *Martyrs of Córdoba*, 300.

24. Ibid., 35, translation by Colbert, *Martyrs of Córdoba*, 301.

25. The literature on this subject is extensive. A few of the relevant books and articles include García Gómez, *Poemas arábigoandaluces*, "Veinticuatro jarŷas romances en muwaššaḥas árabes," and *Las jarchas romances de la serie árabe en su marco;* Jones, "Sunbeams from Cucumbers?"; Monroe, "Pedir peras al olmo?"; and Stern, *Chansons mozarabes.*

26. Ibn Hazm, *Jamharat ansab al-Arab*, 443. Also on the subject of usage of Romance see Ribera y Tarragó, *Disertaciones y opúsculos*, 1:27–56. Most of Ribera y Tarragó's evidence comes from al-Khushani. Al-Khushani's statements about language usage are open to interpretation, but it seems clear that it was fairly unusual for a person of any religion or ethnic group in ninth-century Córdoba to be completely ignorant of Romance.

27. See McKitterick, "Literacy and the Laity in Early Medieval Spain."

28. Ibid.

29. Albar, *Vita Eulogii*, 9.

30. Gil, *Corpus Scriptorum Muzarabicorum*, 2:723–33.

31. Bulliet develops this methodology in *Conversion to Islam in the Medieval Period.*

32. Ibid., 124–28. It is important to note that Bulliet is talking about percentages rather than absolute numbers because by 1200 al-Andalus had lost territory to the Christian north.

33. Ibid., 33–42.

34. Al-Khushani, *Kitab al-qudat bi Qurtuba*, text 125–26, trans. 154–55, tells the story of a man convicted of heresy who was condemned to death by Córdoba's leading *ulama* (religious scholars). The amir and his counselors, however, refused to support the decision. According to Lévi-Provençal, this man had studied in the East and returned to al-Andalus versed in techniques of rational disputation about theological matters (*kalam*), a practice that was frowned upon by the conservative Malikite *ulama* (*Histoire de l'Espagne musulmane*, 1:146–50, 288–89).

35. See Chapter 3.

36. For the basics of Islamic law on mixed marriages, see Levy, *Social Structure of Islam*, 103; Schacht, *Introduction to Islamic Law*, 130–33; and Shukri, *Muhammedan Law*, 30–31.

37. King, *Law and Society in the Visigothic Kingdom*, 222–50. Divorce was prohibited by the church but continued to be available under certain circumstances at least until the time of the Muslim invasion.

38. Shukri, *Muhammedan Law*, 30–31.

39. Eulogius, *Memoriale*, 3.17.

40. Ibid., 3.8. He reports that Felix was of the Gaetuli (*natione Gaetulus*). Gaetuli was a Roman name applied to various tribes living in the Atlas Mountains and the northeast fringes of the Sahara. See *The Cambridge History of Africa*, 2:140–43.

41. Lévi-Provençal, *Histoire de l'Espagne musulmane*, 1:187.

42. Guichard, *Al-Andalus*, 20–23, 55–85, 121–25.

43. Goody, *Development of the Family and Marriage in Europe*, 6–33 and appendix 2.

2. The Martyrs' Movement

1. See particularly Colbert, *Martyrs of Córdoba*, who summarizes Eulogius's remarks about each martyr; also Wolf, *Christian Martyrs*, 23–35.

2. Eulogius, *Memoriale*, 2.8.

3. Ibid., 3.17.

4. The two other *qadis* were Ahmad's brother Muhammad ibn Ziyad, who was appointed by Abd al-Rahman II, and Muhammad's son Al-Habib Ahmad ibn Muhammad ibn Ziyad, appointed by Abd Allah and again by Abd al-Rahman III. See al-Khushani, *Kitab al-qudat bi Qurtuba*, text 100–106,

114-17, 174-82, 188-90, trans. 122-31, 139-43, 215-25, 234-37; Ibn Hayyan, *Al-Muqtabas min anba ahl al-Andalus,* 71-75, also Makki's n. 179; Ibn Hazm, *Jamharat ansab al-Arab,* 422-25.

5. Lévi-Provençal, *Histoire de l'Espagne musulmane,* 1:164-69; Al-Khushani, *Kitab al-qudat bi Qurtuba,* text 69-70, trans. 86-87.

6. Eulogius, *Memoriale,* 2.1. Albar also describes Perfectus's death in the *Indiculus,* 8. The details and the quotation in my account are from Eulogius.

7. Eulogius, *Memoriale,* 2.5.

8. Eulogius, *Apologeticus martyrum,* 16. The biography of Muhammad is discussed in Chapter 3.

9. Eulogius, *Memoriale,* 1.9, and Albar, *Indiculus,* 5. Quotations are from Albar.

10. Albar, *Indiculus,* 9.

11. Eulogius, *Memoriale,* 2.10.

12. Ibid., 1, *praef.,* and 2.2.

13. Watt, in *History of Islamic Spain,* 58, argues that the title *qumis* referred to a tax collector. Simonet, *Historia de los mozárabes,* 111-13, distinguishes between the *qumis* or head of the Christian community and the *exceptor* or tax collector. Lévi-Provençal, *Histoire de l'Espagne musulmane,* 1:164-69, identifies tax collecting as one of *qumis* Rabia's duties. Whatever the precise distinction between the *qumis* and the *exceptor,* it is clear that both were powerful men, were appointed by the amir, and had some responsibility for collecting Christians' taxes.

14. Al-Khushani, *Kitab al-qudat bi Qurtuba,* text 108, trans. 131-32.

15. See especially the *Memoriale,* 2.15, in which Eulogius offers a deeply hostile description of the Christian who was *exceptor* in 851-52; see also Abbot Samson's *Apologeticus,* 2, *praef.,* for a description of conflict between radical and court Christians.

16. See in particular Eulogius, *Memoriale,* 3.10.

17. Ibid., 3.16.

18. Simonet, *Historia de los mozárabes,* 111-13, equates the Latin term *censor* with the Arabic *qadi al-ajam,* or judge of the Christians. That judge had final say over questions of family law, personal status, and commercial transactions within the Christian community. The state had jurisdiction over disputes between Christians and Muslims and most aspects of criminal law. The martyrs were brought before the Muslim *qadi* because they had violated the *dhimma.* See also Goitein, *Mediterranean Society,* 2:2-3.

19. Eulogius, *Memoriale,* 1, *praef.*

20. Simonet, *Historia de los mozárabes,* 327.

21. Eulogius, *Memoriale*, 3.10.

22. Ibid., 2.10. Eulogius also compares the small size of Cordovan monasteries to larger monasteries in northern Spain in *epist.* 3, sect. 2–4 and 10.
On early medieval monasticism in Spain, see Orlandis, "Los monasterios familiares en España" and *Historia de España*, 246–49.

23. Bishko, *Spanish and Portuguese Monastic History*, sect. 1, p. 2.

24. Eulogius, *Memoriale*, 2.4 and 3.10.

25. Collins, *Early Medieval Spain*, 80–87.

26. Nasrallah, *Saint Jean de Damas*, 91–94.

27. Eulogius, *Memoriale*, 2.1.6.

28. Ibid., 2.7.

29. Ibid., 2.8.

30. Eulogius, *Documentum*, 21.

31. Eulogius, *Memoriale*, 2.4.

32. Albar, *Vita Eulogii*, 4–6.

33. Ibid., 4.

34. Eulogius, *Documentum*, 4.

35. The eighth-century jurist al-Shaybani made this ruling. See Khadduri, *Islamic Law of Nations*, 195–229.

36. Ibid., 149–52.

37. Eulogius, *Documentum*, 14.

38. Ibid., 2.

39. Ibid., 1.

40. From the *Liber hebraicarum quaestionum in Genesim;* see Chapter 3.

41. Eulogius, *Documentum*, 20.

42. Ibid., 21. We also find Eulogius caressing Flora's scars in the *Memoriale*, 2.8.8.

43. Eulogius, *Documentum*, 20–21.

44. Eulogius, *Memoriale*, 2.10.

45. Eulogius uses only her Christian name, Sabigotho. The name Nathalia is used in Aimoin's account of the translation of Aurelius's and Sabigotho's relics to France.

46. Eulogius, *Apologeticus martyrum*, 21–29.

47. Albar, *Vita Eulogii*, 13–16.

48. Eulogius, *Epist.* 3.12.

49. This technique of rule through community leaders is addressed in Mottahedeh, *Loyalty and Leadership in Early Islamic Society;* Lapidus, *Muslim Cities in the Later Middle Ages;* and Bulliet, *Patricians of Nishapur.*

50. Eulogius, *Memoriale*, 2.16.2.

51. Ibid., 2.15. The Visigothic kings claimed the right to convoke episcopal councils so the Muslim amirs may in part have inherited this tradition from their predecessors.

52. Eulogius, *Memoriale*, 3.4.

53. Ibid., 3.5, 3.7. It is certainly possible that Muhammad I entertained such a plan, but rumors about an impending massacre are standard in *dhimmi* writing. Lewis cites an almost identical story told by a sixteenth-century archbishop of Corfu, in which the Ottoman Sultan Murad III threatened to execute all the *dhimmis* under his rule but was dissuaded by his mother and a trusted adviser (*Jews of Islam,* 51). In neither case did a massacre take place. Whether or not the rulers' intentions were serious, however, such rumors reveal how precarious *dhimmis* felt their situation to be in times of crisis.

54. Goitein, *Mediterranean Society,* 2:286–87.

55. Eulogius, *Memoriale*, 2.14.

56. Ibid., 3.7.

57. Ibid., 2.15, 3.2.

58. Ibid., 1, *Epistula ad Albarum.*

59. Albar, *Indiculus*, 14.

60. Two unnamed sisters died in 861 (Aimoin, *De translatione,* 540–41); an anonymous Christian confessor was questioned by the *qadi* in 920 (al-Khushani, *Kitab al-qudat bi Qurtuba,* text 186–87, trans. 231–33); an inscription refers to the martyrdom of a woman named Eugenia in 923 (Flórez et al., *España sagrada,* 10:462–65); the martyr Pelagius died in 925 (ibid., 23:106–11, 231–46); and Vulfura and Argentea, who may have been the daughters of the *muwallad* (Iberian Muslim) rebel Umar Ibn Hafsun, were executed in 931 (ibid., 10:465–71, 564–70).

3. Eulogius and Albar

1. Albar, *Vita Eulogii,* 2.

2. Ibid., 15.

3. Eulogius, *Memoriale*, 3.7.

4. Albar, *Vita Eulogii,* 8.

5. Ibid., 9.

6. Ibid., 4.

7. Ibid., 8.

8. Ibid., 2; Eulogius, *Memoriale*, 2.7.

9. Albar, *Vita Eulogii,* 3, 5.

10. Eulogius, *Epist.* 3.

11. Eulogius, *Memoriale*, 3.4–5.

12. Albar, *Vita Eulogii*, 1.

13. Albar, *Epist*. 18.

14. Ibid., 9, 11, 12, and 13 contain references to Albar's penance.

15. Watkins, *History of Penance*, 2:564–65.

16. Albar, *Epist*. 11–13.

17. Ibid., 9.

18. Samson, *Apologeticus*, 2, *praef.*, 6.

19. Eulogius, *Memoriale*, 2.10.

20. Sahas, in his *John of Damascus*, 32–33, suggests this approximate date for the Arabic biography of John.

21. Ibid., 17–48, sketches the major events of John's life. See also Nasrallah, *Saint Jean de Damas*, 71–103.

22. Sahas, *John of Damascus*, 41–45. Nasrallah, *Saint Jean de Damas*, 74–75, places John's retirement from government earlier, arguing that Umar II (717–20) ordered that all Christians be eliminated from government positions. Sahas follows the dating of the earliest Greek *vita* of John.

23. Theophanes the Confessor, *Chronographia*, cited in Sahas, *John of Damascus*, 68–69.

24. Fábrega Grau, *Pasionario hispánico*.

25. On this issue of Eulogius's use of earlier martyrologies see also Wolf, *Christian Martyrs*, 77–104.

26. Fábrega Grau, *Pasionario hispánico*, 2:25–40.

27. Ibid., 176–82; Eulogius, *Memoriale*, 2.7.

28. *Liber hebraicarum quaestionum in Genesim*, in Migne et al., *Patrologiae Cursus Completus*, 23:935–1009.

29. Jerome, *Epist*. 22 to Eustochium, in Migne et al., *Patrologiae*, 22:394–425; Eulogius, *Documentum*, 2.

30. Eulogius, *Documentum*, 1.

31. Text and translation from Prudentius, *Peristephanon*, 2:146–47.

32. Eulogius, *Memoriale*, 3.11.

33. Eulogius, *Documentum*, 4.

34. Prudentius, *Peristephanon*, 2:338–45; the Ambrose work is in Migne, *Patrologiae*, 15:549–727. At least some of Ambrose's works were available to the Cordovan authors; Samson in particular quotes from Ambrose's *De fide*.

35. Riddle, in *The Martyrs*, 55–60, emphasizes that during the Roman persecutions, oral and written accounts of earlier martyrdoms helped potential martyrs to learn their roles—how to reply to the magistrate's questions, for example, and how to conduct themselves in the arena.

36. Eulogius, *Apologeticus martyrum*, 12.

37. Ibid., 5.

38. Eulogius, *Memoriale*, 2.12, 2.1.

39. Albar, *Vita Eulogii*, 15-16.

40. Eulogius, *Memoriale*, 1.13-17; *Apologeticus martyrum*, 3.7-9.

41. Wolf, *Christian Martyrs*, 82-83, makes the point that a tradition of miracles grows up when there is consensus in the community that they happened. Clearly there was no such consensus among Cordovan Christians.

42. Albar, *Indiculus*, 6.

43. Ibid., 3-4, 14.

44. Eulogius, *Apologeticus martyrum*, 16.

45. Albar, *Indiculus*, 9; Eulogius, *Apologeticus martyrum*, 12.

46. "Isa," *Encyclopedia of Islam*.

47. Sura 19.

48. In Sura 19.35 he is called "*qawl al-haqq*," the true word or the speech of God, and in 3.46 an angel tells Mary that God sends her tidings of "a word from him" (*bi kalimatin minhu*).

49. Eulogius, *Apologeticus martyrum*, 19; *Memoriale*, 1.7.

50. Albar, *Indiculus*, 9.

51. Colbert, *Martyrs of Córdoba*, 158, believes it was written around 851. Speraindeo's letter, along with Albar's letter requesting his teacher's advice, appear in Gil, *Corpus Scriptorum*, 1:201-10, as Albar, *Epist.* 7 and 8; the correspondence also appears in Migne et al., *Patrologiae*, 115:959-66.

52. Franz R. Franke, in "Die freiwilligen Märtyrer," argues that the "heresy" under discussion is Islam. Neither Speraindeo nor Albar mentions Islam, though, and Speraindeo, in talking about the heretics, says that one should treat a fallen brother with compassion, a remark he would not be likely to make about Muslims.

53. Albar quotes from several anti-Adoptionist treatises in these letters. The Adoptionist controversy in al-Andalus is outlined in Colbert, *Martyrs of Córdoba*, 64-85; Menéndez y Pelayo, *Historia de los heterodoxos españoles*, 273-92; and Simonet, *Historia de los mozárabes*, 266-77.

54. The various theories about Adoptionism's origins are outlined in Rivera, *Elipando de Toledo*, 29-40. Rivera suggests that Elipandus had some Muslim education.

55. Adeney, *Greek and Eastern Churches*, 92-101.

56. Eulogius, *Apologeticus martyrum*, 16. Elements of this biography of Muhammad turn up in later Spanish writing (see the *Primera crónica general*, chaps.

468–94) but did not influence other Western anti-Islamic polemic. The story does not appear to have a Middle Eastern precursor. See Daniel, *Islam and the West*, 5–6, and Franke, "Die freiwilligen Märtyrer," 38–47.

57. Albar, *Indiculus*, 23–24.

58. Ibid., 28, 31, 33.

59. Franke, "Die freiwilligen Märtyrer," 135–41.

60. *Concerning Heresies*, translation in Sahas, *John of Damascus*, Appendix 1, 132–41.

61. Eulogius, *Apologeticus martyrum*, 19.

62. Albar, *Indiculus*, 25.

63. Ibid., 27. The quotation is from *Moralia in Job*, in Migne et al., *Patrologiae*, 75:509–1162.

64. Eulogius, *Memoriale*, 1.21; Albar, *Indiculus*, 6.

65. Eulogius, *Memoriale*, 1.21.

66. Albar, *Indiculus*, 31.

67. See Hodgson, "A Comparison of Islam and Christianity."

68. Al-Khushani, *Kitab al-qudat bi Qurtuba*, text 186–87, trans. 231–33.

69. Eulogius, *Memoriale*, 2.13.

70. Albar, *Vita Eulogii*, 10.

71. A description of the journey appears in book 1 of Aimoin's *De translatione*.

72. Ibid., 3.28.

73. The miracle stories appear in Aimoin, books 2 and 3.

74. Heffernan, in *Sacred Biography*, 31–37, describes the gradual process by which stories about saints often move from local oral tradition to conflicting written versions to a single written version which people generally recognize as legitimate. The fact that Eulogius was writing as events in Córdoba were still unfolding may have made it more difficult for him to develop consensus in the community.

4. Christians as the Enemy

1. Albar, *Indiculus*, 5.

2. Ibid., 9.

3. Eulogius, *Memoriale*, 2.15.

4. Albar, *Indiculus*, 35.

5. Samson gives information about the court in his *Apologeticus*, 2, *praef.*

6. Ibid.

7. Albar, *Indiculus*, 35.

8. Ibid.

9. Abbot John of St. Arnulf, *Vita Johannis abbatis Gorziensis*, 372.

10. Samson, *Apologeticus*, 2.7.

11. Samson reports Hostegesis's arguments in 2.3; he refutes them in 2.7–27.

12. Ibid., 2.7.

13. Albar, *Vita Eulogii*, 4.

14. Ibid., 6.

15. Ibid., 4; Eulogius, *Memoriale*, 2.16.

16. Aimoin puts Saul back in Córdoba by 858, but he may have returned sooner.

17. Albar, *Epist.* 11–13.

18. Ibid., 12.

19. Colbert, *Martyrs of Córdoba*, 321–32, describes the scholarly theories regarding letter 10. He believes that Reccafred wrote the letter, which seems unlikely; the letter was written by someone who was modifying his views about events in Córdoba, and there is no indication that Reccafred ever held views favorable to the martyrs.

20. Albar, *Indiculus*, 16–17.

21. Migetius's beliefs are described by Bishop Elipandus of Toledo, *Epistula in Migetium*, in Gil, *Corpus Scriptorum*, 1:68–78; see especially sections 10–11. Discussions of Migetianism can be found in Colbert, *Martyrs of Córdoba*, 55–63; Menéndez y Pelayo, *Historia de los heterodoxos españoles*, 271–73; and Simonet, *Historia de los mozárabes*, 264–65.

22. The Acts of the Council of 839 appear in Gil, *Corpus Scriptorum*, 1:135–41. See especially sections 2, 4, and 6. See also Colbert, *Martyrs of Córdoba*, 135–39; Menéndez y Pelayo, *Historia de los heterodoxos españoles*, 312–13; Simonet, *Historia de los mozárabes*, 371–73.

23. The Council of 839 accused Cassians of abstaining "from the food of the gentiles" (*ab escis gentilium*). Although Christians in al-Andalus often use the word "gentiles" to refer to Muslims, in this case I believe the best interpretation is that Cassians rejected "gentile" food in the sense of food that violated Jewish law.

24. Albar, *Indiculus*, 3.

25. Ibid., 18.

26. Ibid., 33.

27. Eulogius, *Memoriale, praef.*

28. Recemudus's mission to the Byzantines is described in Liutprand of Cremona, *Antapodosis*.

29. The best edition of the calendar is by Reinhardt Dozy, *Le calendrier*

de Cordoue, translated and revised by Charles Pellat. Al-Maqqari, *Nafh al-tib,* 2:169, identifies Recemundus, or Rabi ibn Zayd as he was called in Arabic, as the author and reports that the calendar was presented to al-Hakam.

30. Flórez et al., *España sagrada,* 23:106–11, 231–46.

31. Recemundus's authorship of both versions is not accepted by all scholars, although I believe it is the conclusion that best fits the evidence. Pellat discusses other theories about the origins of the two versions in the introduction to his edition.

5. The Martyrs

1. Eulogius, *Memoriale,* 2.15.

2. Franke, "Die freiwilligen Märtyrer," 19–25, emphasizes the issue of penance; Wolf, *Christian Martyrs,* 107–19, argues that martyrdom was a natural extension of the confessors' asceticism.

3. *De ecclesiasticis officiis,* 2.17, quoted in Watkins, *History of Penance,* 2:572–73.

4. Eulogius, *Memoriale,* 1.1.

5. Ibid., 2.10.

6. Ibid., 3.4.

7. Ibid., 2.8.

8. Ibid., 3.8.

9. Ibid., 1, *praef.,* and 2.2.

10. Sura 9.29.

11. Goitein, *Mediterranean Society,* 2:375.

12. Eulogius, *Memoriale,* 3.16.

13. Nasrallah, *Saint Jean de Damas,* 72–75; Shaban, *Islamic History,* 111–17, 132–37.

14. Albar, *Vita Eulogii,* 13–16.

15. Eulogius, *Apologeticus martyrum,* 21–25.

16. Eulogius, *Memoriale,* 2.10.

17. Ibid., 2.7.

18. Ibid., 2.8.

19. Albar, *Indiculus,* 6.

20. Eulogius, *Memoriale,* 3.17.

21. Ibid., 3.10.

22. Bynum discusses in *Holy Feast and Holy Fast,* 219–44, how medieval women used ascetic practices (especially fasting) as a means of asserting control over their environment.

23. Eulogius, *Documentum,* 20–21.

6. Problems of Religious and Cultural Identity

1. See, for example, Ullman, *Transformed Self*. As a psychologist, Ullman understands conversion as a personal transformation brought about by emotional needs and psychological stress.

2. Bulliet discusses the social and cultural dimensions of conversion to Islam in his *Conversion to Islam*, 33–42.

Changes in religious affiliation can, of course, be tied to changes in cultural and legal status in the modern world as well as in the Middle Ages. For a theoretical discussion of these issues in a modern context see Suad Joseph, "Muslim-Christian Conflicts: A Theoretical Perspective," in Joseph and Pillsbury, eds., *Muslim-Christian Conflicts*, 1–60.

3. Acts 15.1–5, 16.3; 1 Cor. 7.18; Rom. 2.25–29.

4. "Circumcision (*khitan*)," *Encyclopedia of Islam*.

5. Samson, *Apologeticus*, 2, praef., 2, accuses courtiers of participating in drinking parties. As an antiassimilationist Christian, Samson is not an objective source of information, but Islamic court culture in this period did encourage practices that were not always compatible with Islamic law. The ninth-century Abbasid court poetry of Abu Nuwas, for example, celebrated winedrinking and homosexual love.

6. Lévi-Provençal, *Histoire de l'Espagne musulmane*, 1:267–68. See also Watt, *History of Islamic Spain*, 52–57.

7. Mottahedeh, *Loyalty and Leadership*, 98–104; Watt, *History of Islamic Spain*, 66–67.

8. Ibn al-Qutiyya, *Tarikh ifitah al-Andulus*, 96.

9. Al-Khushani, *Kitab al-qudat bi Qurtuba*, text 24–26, 161–63; trans. 31–33, 200–202.

10. Eulogius, *Memoriale*, 1, praef., and 2.2. See also the story of Ibn Antonian below.

11. Al-Khushani describes a case in which a speaker of Romance (*ajami al-lisan*) brings a complaint before the amir's officials; Romance was apparently known at court (*Kitab al-qudat bi Qurtuba*, text 94–97, trans. 116–19).

12. Pahlavi, the ancient literary form of Persian, became restricted to Zoroastrian liturgical uses after the Muslim invasion. The new Persian literary language that eventually emerged was Dari; originally a southwestern dialect, it spread throughout the Persian world and became an important language of high culture in the tenth century. Dari was written in Arabic script and was influenced by Arabic syntax and loan worlds. See Hodgson, *Venture of Islam*, 280–314; Lapidus, *Islamic Societies*, 91–92, 152–61; "Iran, Literature," *Encyclopedia of Islam*.

13. Bulliet, *Conversion to Islam*, 114–15.

14. It was, however, open to influence from popular culture, as is outlined in Chapter 1.

15. Al-Khushani, *Kitab al-qudat bi Qurtuba*, text 117–26, 141–45, trans. 144–55, 175–77; Ibn al-Qutiyya, *Tarikh iftah al-Andalus*, 86–88.

16. Ibn al-Qutiyya, *Tarikh iftah al-Andalus*, 88.

17. Al-Khushani describes the conflict with Hashim; Ibn al-Qutiyya refers only to the charge of theft.

18. Al-Khushani, *Kitab al-qudat bi Qurtuba*, text 117–18, trans. 144.

19. Ibn Antonian's story appears in Ibn Hayyan, *Al-Muqtabas min anba ahl al-Andalus*, 138–42; Ibn al-Qutiyya, *Tarikh iftah al-Andalus*, 95–98; Al-Khushani, *Kitab al-qudat bi Qurtuba*, text 130–34, trans. 159–64. The Latin sources do not mention him by name, but he is probably the government official and recent convert to Islam whom Eulogius describes as the *exceptor rei publicae* in the *Memoriale*, 2.15 and 3.2.

20. Medieval Islamic governments generally employed *dhimmi*s or recent converts as translators between Islamic and Western languages. Most Muslims regarded the study of non-Islamic languages as demeaning. See Lewis, *Muslim Discovery of Europe*, 71–88.

21. Eulogius, *Memoriale*, 3.2. Because Islamic law did not, strictly speaking, permit *dhimmi*s in positions of power, *dhimmi* bureaucrats were subject to occasional purges throughout the Islamic world in this period. Fiey in *Chrétiens syriaques sous les Abbassides*, 26–28 and 30–39, gives examples of mass dismissals of *dhimmi*s from the Abbasid government.

22. The phrase Ibn al-Qutiyya uses is "*shajiya bi-hi.*"

23. Ibn al-Qutiyya, *Tarikh iftah al-Andalus*, 96. Robert C. Stacey, in his "The Conversion of Jews to Christianity in Thirteenth-Century England," describes the similar situation of Jewish converts to Christianity who worked for the government in thirteenth-century England: they could rise to high positions of authority but were never treated as equal to "real" Christians.

24. Only al-Khushani describes Hashim's suit against Ibn Antonian's estate.

25. Lapidus, *History of Islamic Societies*, 45–53.

26. Shaban, *Abbasid Revolution*, 138–68.

27. Abd al-Malik (692–705) and al-Walid I (705–15) in particular promoted Arabic as the language of government and public life. See Shaban, *Islamic History*, 100–126.

28. Lapidus, *Islamic Societies*, 126–61.

Bibliography

Aimoin. *De translatione SS. martyrum Georgii monachi, Aurelii, et Nathaliae.* In Migne et al., 115:939–60.

Adeney, Walter F. *The Greek and Eastern Churches.* New York: C. Scribner's Sons, 1908.

Albar, Paul. *Epistulae.* In Gil, 1:144–270.

———. *Indiculus luminosus.* In Gil, 1:270–315.

———. *Vita Eulogii.* In Gil, 1:330–43.

Al-Baladhuri. *The Origins of the Islamic State.* Translated by Philip Hitti. New York: Columbia UP, 1916.

Barbero, Abilio, and Marcelo Vigil. *Sobre los orígenes sociales de la Reconquista.* Barcelona: Editorial Ariel, 1974.

Bishko, C. J. *Spanish and Portuguese Monastic History, 600–1300.* London: Variorum Reprints, 1984.

Broom, Leonard, et al. "Acculturation: An Exploratory Formulation." *American Anthropologist* 56 (1954): 973–1000.

Bulliet, Richard W. *Conversion to Islam in the Medieval Period.* Cambridge: Harvard UP, 1979.

———. *The Patricians of Nishapur.* Cambridge: Harvard UP, 1972.

Bynum, Caroline Walker. *Holy Feast and Holy Fast.* Berkeley: U of California P, 1987.

Cagigas, Isidro de las. *Los mozárabes.* 2 vols. Madrid, 1947–48.

The Cambridge History of Africa. 8 vols. Edited by J. D. Fage and Roland Oliver. Cambridge and New York, 1975–.

Colbert, Edward P. *The Martyrs of Córdoba (850–859): A Study of the Sources.* Washington DC: Catholic U of America P, 1962.

Collins, Roger. *The Arab Conquest of Spain.* Cambridge, Mass.: Basil Blackwell, 1989.

———. *Early Medieval Spain.* New York: St. Martin's, 1983.

———, ed. *Law, Culture, and Regionalism in Early Medieval Spain.* Hampshire: Variorum Reprints, 1992.

Daniel, Norman. *Islam and the West: The Making of an Image.* Edinburgh: Edinburgh UP, 1960.

Dozy, Reinhardt. *Le calendrier de Cordoue.* Translated and revised by Charles Pellat. Leiden: Brill, 1961.

———. *Histoire des musulmans d'Espagne.* 3 vols. Revised by Evariste Lévi-Provençal. Leiden: Brill, 1932.

Encyclopedia of Islam. Edited by E. Van Donzel, B. Lewis, and Ch. Pellat. Leiden, 1978.

Eulogius. *Documentum martyriale.* In Gil, 2:459–75.

———. *Epistulae.* In Gil, 2:495–503.

———. *Liber apologeticus martyrum.* In Gil, 2:475–95.

———. *Memoriale sanctorum.* In Gil, 2:363–459.

Fábrega Grau, Ángel, ed. 2 vols. *Pasionario hispánico. Monumenta Hispaniae sacra, serie liturgica, 6.* Madrid, 1950.

Fiey, Jean Maurice. *Chrétiens syriaques sous les Abbassides.* Louvain, 1980.

Flórez, Enrique, et al. *España sagrada.* 52 vols. Madrid, 1747–1918.

Franke, Franz R. "Die freiwilligen Märtyrer von Cordova und das Verhältnis des Mozarabes zum Islam." *Gesammelte Aufsätze zur Kulturgeschichte Spaniens* 13 (1958):1–170.

Frend, W. H. C. *Martyrdom and Persecution in the Early Church.* Oxford: Blackwell, 1965.

Fyzee, Asaf. *Outlines of Muhammadan Law.* Oxford: Oxford UP, 1964.

García Gómez, Emilio. *Las jarchas romances de la serie árabe en su marco.* Madrid: Socieded de Estudios y Publicaciones, 1965.

———. *Poemas arábigoandaluces.* Madrid: Editorial Plutarco, 1940.

———. "Veinticuatro jaryas romances en muwaššaḥas árabes." *Al-Andalus* 17 (1952): 57–127.

Gil, Juan. *Corpus Scriptorum Muzarabicorum.* 2 vols. Madrid, 1973.

Glick, Thomas. *Islamic and Christian Spain in the Early Middle Ages.* Princeton: Princeton UP, 1979.

Glick, Thomas, and Oriol Pi-Sunyer. "Acculturation as an Explanatory Concept in Spanish History." *Comparative Studies in Society and History* 11 (1969): 136–54.

Goitein, S. D. *A Mediterranean Society.* 4 vols. Berkeley and Los Angeles: U of California P, 1971.

Goody, Jack. *The Development of the Family and Marriage in Europe.* Cambridge: Cambridge UP, 1983.

Grabar, Oleg. *The Formation of Islamic Art.* New Haven: Yale UP, 1973.

Guichard, Pierre. *Al-Andalus.* Barcelona: Barral Editores, 1976.

Heffernan, Thomas. *Sacred Biography.* Oxford: Oxford UP, 1988.

Hillgarth, J. N. "Popular Religion in Visigothic Spain." In *Visigothic Spain,* edited by Edward James, pp. 3–60. Oxford: Oxford UP, 1980.

Hodgson, Marshall G. S. "A Comparison of Islam and Christianity as Frameworks for the Religious Life." *Diogenes* 32 (1960): 49–74.

———. *The Venture of Islam.* 3 vols. Chicago: U of Chicago P, 1974.

Ibn Hayyan. *Al-Muqtabas min anba ahl al-Andalus.* Edited by Mahmud Ali Makki. Beirut, 1973.

Ibn Hazm. *Jamharat ansab al-Arab.* Beirut, 1983.

Ibn al-Qutiyya. *Tarikh iftitah al-Andalus.* Edited by Ibrahim al-Abyari. Cairo and Beirut, 1982.

John, Abbot of St. Arnulf. *Vita Johannis abbatis Gorziensis.* Edited by George H. Pertz. In *Monumenta Germaniae Historica, Scriptores,* 4:335–77. Hanover, 1841.

Jones, Alan. "Sunbeams from Cucumbers? An Arabist's Assessment of the State of *Kharja* Studies." *La Corónica* 10 (1981): 38–53.

Joseph, Suad, and Barbara Pillsbury, eds. *Muslim-Christian Conflicts: Economic, Political, and Social Origins.* Boulder CO: Westview, 1978.

Khadduri, Majid. *The Islamic Law of Nations.* Baltimore: Johns Hopkins UP, 1966.

Al-Khushani. *Kitab al-qudat bi Qurtuba.* Edited and translated by Julián Ribera y Tarragó. Madrid, 1914.

King, P. D. *Law and Society in the Visigothic Kingdom.* Cambridge: Cambridge UP, 1972.

Lambert, Elie. "Le voyage de saint Euloge dans les Pyrénées en 848." In *Estudios dedicados a Menéndez Pidal,* 7:557–67. Madrid: Consejo Superior de Investigaciones Científicas, 1953.

Lapidus, Ira M. *A History of Islamic Societies.* Cambridge: Cambridge UP, 1988.

———. *Muslim Cities in the Later Middle Ages.* Cambridge: Harvard UP, 1967.

Leovigildus. *De habitu clericorum.* In Gil, 2:667–84.

Lévi-Provençal, Evariste. *Histoire de l'Espagne musulmane.* 3 vols. Paris: G. P. Maisonneuve et Larose, 1950.

Levy, Reuben. *The Social Structure of Islam*. Cambridge: Cambridge UP, 1957.

Lewis, Bernard. *The Jews of Islam*. Princeton: Princeton UP, 1984.

————. *The Muslim Discovery of Europe*. New York: W. W. Norton, 1982.

Liutprand of Cremona. *Antapodosis*. Edited by Joseph Becker. In *Monumenta Germaniae Historica, Scriptores . . . in usum scholarum*, pp. 1–158. Hanover, 1915.

Al-Maqqari, *Nafh al-tib*. 8 vols. Edited by Ihsan Abbas. Beirut, 1968.

McKitterick, R. "Literacy and the Laity in Early Medieval Spain." In Collins, ed., *Law, Culture, and Regionalism*, section 15.

Menéndez y Pelayo, Marcelino. *Historia de los heterodoxos españoles*. Madrid: Librería católica de San Jose, 1880.

Migne, J. P., et al. *Patrologiae Cursus Completus, Series Latina*. Paris, 1944–66.

Monroe, James. "Pedir peras al olmo? On Medieval Arabs and Modern Arabists." *La Corónica* 10 (1982): 121–47.

————. *The Shu'ubiyya in Al-Andalus*. Berkeley and Los Angeles: U of California P, 1970.

Mottahedeh, Roy. *Loyalty and Leadership in Early Islamic Society*. Princeton: Princeton UP, 1980.

Nasrallah, P. Joseph. *Saint Jean de Damas, son époque—sa vie—son oeuvre*. Harissa, 1950.

Orlandis, José. *Estudios sobre instituciones monásticas medievales*. Pamplona: Universidad de Navarra, 1971.

————. *Historia de España: La España visigótica*. Madrid: Gredos, 1977.

————. "Los monasterios familiares en España durante la alta edad media." *Anuario de historia del derecho español* 26 (1956): 5–46.

Prudentius. *Peristephanon*. In H. J. Thomson, *Prudentius*, Loeb Classical Library. London, 1953.

Ribera y Tarragó, Julián. *Disertaciones y opúsculos*. 2 vols. Madrid, 1928.

Riddle, Donald W. *The Martyrs: A Study in Social Control*. Chicago: U of Chicago P, 1931.

Rivera, Juan Francisco. *Elipando de Toledo*. Toledo: Editorial Católica Toledana, 1939.

Sage, Carleton M. *Paul Albar of Cordoba: Studies on his Life and Writings*. Washington DC: Catholic U of America P, 1943.

Sahas, Daniel J. *John of Damascus on Islam*. Leiden: Brill, 1972.

Samson. *Apologeticus*. In Gil, 2:506–658.

Sánchez Albornoz, Claudio. *España, un enigma histórico*. Buenos Aires: Editorial Sudamericana, 1956.

Schacht, Joseph. *An Introduction to Islamic Law*. Oxford: Clarendon, 1964.

Shaban, M. A. *The Abbasid Revolution*. Cambridge: Cambridge UP, 1970.

————. *Islamic History: A New Interpretation*. Cambridge: Cambridge UP, 1971.

Shukri, Ahmed. *Muhammedan Law of Marriage and Divorce*. New York: AMS Press, 1966.

Simonet, Francisco Javier. *Glosario de voces ibéricas y latinas usadas entre los mozárabes*. Madrid, 1888.

————. *Historia de los mozárabes de España*. Madrid, 1897.

Stacey, Robert C. "The Conversion of Jews to Christianity in Thirteenth-Century England." *Speculum* 67 (1992): 263–83.

Stern, S. M. *Les chansons mozarabes: Les vers finaux (Kharjas) en espagnol dans les muwashshahs arabes et hébreux*. Oxford: Bruno Cassirer, 1964.

Taha, Abdulwahid Dhanun. *The Muslim Conquest and Settlement of North Africa and Spain*. London: Routledge, 1989.

Tritton, A. S. *The Caliphs and Their Non-Muslim Subjects*. London: F. Cass, 1930.

Ullman, Chana. *The Transformed Self: The Psychology of Religious Conversion*. New York: Plenum, 1989.

Waltz, James. "The Significance of the Voluntary Martyrs of Ninth-Century Córdoba." *Muslim World* 60 (1970): 143–59, 226–36.

Wasserstein, David. *The Rise and Fall of the Party Kings*. Princeton: Princeton UP, 1985.

Watkins, Oscar D. *A History of Penance*. 2 vols. New York: B. Franklin, 1961.

Watt, William Montgomery. *A History of Islamic Spain*. Edinburgh: Edinburgh UP, 1965.

Wellhausen, Julius. *The Arab Kingdom and Its Fall*. Translated by Margaret Weir. Beirut: Khayats, 1963.

Wolf, Kenneth Baxter. *Christian Martyrs in Muslim Spain*. Cambridge: Cambridge UP, 1988.

Ye'or, Bat. *The Dhimmi*. Translated by David Maisel, Paul Fenton, and David Littman. Rutherford NJ: Farleigh Dickinson UP, 1985.

Ziegler, Aloysius K. *Church and State in Visigothic Spain*. Washington DC: Catholic U of America P, 1930.

Index